Zen Jiu Jitsu

Oliver S. Staark

ISBN-13: 978-1479237609
ISBN-10: 1479237604

Second Edition

http://jiujitsubuddha.com

CONTENTS

ACKNOWLEDGMENTS

I would like to thank Carlos and Helio Gracie for their development of a martial art that has brought so much joy (and frustration) into my life. My family, especially my wife, for understanding my obsession during the writing of this book.

The BJJ community as a whole for being such a cool family to be part of. I've never come across so many friendly people willing share ideas and make this sport better for the greater good.

Dan Anderson for his ideas on Monitoring, Bruce Lee and Joe Lewis for their ideas on Modern Martial Arts and what that should mean. My teammates and training partners over the years. Fred Jose my first martial arts instructor for starting this whole thing.

Cover photo courtesy of iStockphoto.com
The image of Batman and Robin is © DC Comics and Warner and credited to www.tapordiecompany.com

INTRODUCTION

Struggle. That's the first word that comes to mind when I think about the transition from Blue Belt to Purple Belt. For reasons that I can't quite work out, when I came to the later stages of being a Blue belt I felt confused and lost in my game. Trying to put all the pieces together seemed like a task too far and quitting looked like an option, after all, most guys my age are hitting the golf course or surfing not rolling on the floor with sweat soaked people. This quitting idea seemed an option at least.

In an effort to review what I was doing and pushing through this plateau I developed a few habits that not only brought about a huge change in my game but by applying them on a consistent basis turned me into a respected player in my academy. From obscurity to recognition even from much higher ranked and established fighters.

So what happened?

Several things, which I will outline in the following pages. The most important being that I gave myself a deadline to get my game together or call it a day. That was significant in that I tried really hard in the period of time I gave myself, and then an injury kept me out for a short time to review. During this time a realization struck me that 30 days was an optimal time to develop this idea.

Since then I have experimented with longer and shorter periods but to make consistent gains while avoiding unnecessary injury it turns out that 30 days is ideal. If you are younger than forty then you might want to experiment with longer, more consistent, periods but for my age-range this worked very well.

Then I made a realization, more a remembrance. When I was younger I trained and competed in the National Freestyle Karate Championships each year. In 1987 I had my best tournament ever, I was in shape and ready to rock. I recalled the training I went through to get to that stage, dragged out all my old notebooks and then followed the steps with BJJ instead of Karate, overlaying the protocol used onto this new framework of grappling.

The system was simple and straightforward. It's actually stupid-simple. No need for fancy techniques or spinning flying anything. Just a modicum of dedication, correct attitude and your BJJ game will flourish. Simple right?

Follow the steps enclosed and you'll make progress. I guarantee it.

What's involved?

This is the book I wish I had when I first started Brazilian Jiu Jitsu quite a few years back. Just like all newbies I was obsessed with finding the next 'cool' technique on YouTube - a site where a few minutes can be lost into days.

As I recall, when I started my coaches taught me the closed guard, the half guard, open guard and various other guards but it was only much later in my development that I actually understood that the guard should be used to control distance and that's pretty much it, control the distance between you and your partner to set up a position. Position leads to transition which leads to submission.

This should have been so fundamental that my progress would have accelerated by months if not years had I made (or my coaches pointed out) this simple distinction. But the nature of BJJ is very visual. We have the techniques demonstrated, the details covered, we drill and then we roll. And mainly because rolling is such great fun we roll around in some kind of aimless human stew until we either improve or get injured and wash out the system.

This is what brought me to put these notes together that soon became a manual. In the last few of years I have developed a way of training that moved me from a mediocre blue belt to a well rounded and accomplished purple belt with most of the improvements coming in the last year. Even as a brown belt I have used these concepts to great effect with some refinements that don't need to be discussed at this stage.

I would even go as far as to say that my current progress is getting even better. What's the big idea? What's the breakthrough? Three things:

- Philosophy
- Psychology
- Attitude

Notice that there's no mention of submissions and this is most certainly not a tap or snap instructional. There are some great books already available that cover that. In fact, there are no photos (or very few), it's all text ... and it's all the stuff that instructors, coaches and professors would love to impart to their students but don't have the time in a traditional 90 minute BJJ lesson.

Let's face it, if you showed up at the academy, kimono in hand and then realized that your professor had a few desks set up on the mat as he began telling you that 'today we are going to cover a few changes to your mind set that will improve your Jiu Jitsu game beyond measure' (see the Chapter on Psychology). You would probably be a selection of:

A. Astounded by his progressive thinking and ready to learn, sharpie in hand.
B. Disappointed, as you wanted a good sweaty workout.
C. Really pissed off because you wanted to choke little Frank who you've disliked since you were a white belt.
D. You hate this classroom garbage, even at high school. Let's go for a beer instead.
E. A combination of the above.

... So, in essence, we actually lose out by learning and drilling. Sounds counter intuitive, right? But if we are learning and drilling so many different techniques that none of them stick then we can never improve, at best we become mediocre and at worst we become confused. Imagine a golf coach teaching a student a new swing (or two) and drilling it then moving to a new swing style the following week!

This coach wouldn't be long for that clubhouse.

Don't misunderstand me, technique and drilling are essential and form a central pillar to my own training method but we cannot ignore the most important area of your game - your brain!

This is one of the reasons I decided to put this together. I am a scholar of Brazilian Jiu Jitsu and an accomplished writer. During the many hours on the mat and the diligence in researching the many topics contained herein I thought it appropriate to pass these ideas along to the BJJ community. If this helps just one person stay on the jiu jitsu path then it's mission accomplished as far as I'm concerned.

Listening to an interview with the Mendes Brothers recently, a question was posed: "Does a coach have to be a World Champion to be a good coach?" Their answer was interesting. They are multiple times world champions so it's important to them and their coaching abilities to agree (being BJJ geniuses doesn't hurt either) but they also stated that their own coach does not compete because 'he doesn't like the feeling'. This was an interesting point and one I completely understand.

I am one of "those guys" ... an 'I don't like the feeling' guy.

Do I compete? Yes. Have I won? Yes. In fact I have pretty much placed in all the various disciplines that I have endeavored to compete in. BJJ though felt very different to me.

I was a competitive Karate player when I was younger, sure I got nervous but I shrugged it off and plowed on. Walking onto the mat at a BJJ event felt much worse. It was a crushing pressure and was so alien to me it freaked me out, 'I just didn't like the feeling'! I wanted to say to my opponent 'sorry my friend, I've made a huge mistake, I'm leaving now, enjoy the rest of the tournament' but I didn't.

Regardless of your hours of sparring and however many teammates you tapped last week, walking into the unknown fills most of us with dread. This is a feeling that may never leave... there are techniques though that can alleviate the pressure a little (see the chapter on Zoning) and these have changed my perspective at a tournament level and even more so in the academy.

Follow the Path

Consistency and Attitude create Ability. These are not, generally speaking, areas we spend too much time on. The three 'A's:

- Attitude, plus
- Attendance, equals
- Ability

I know that some are born with ability, which goes without saying, and I'm not one of them. With the right attitude and an attendance card to be proud of, a good Jiu Jitsu player you can become. (That sounded a bit like Yoda).

So follow my journey young padawan. I will outline in detail the mental techniques that have helped me improve beyond measure ... and some of the tools I used along the way. I am not in any way affiliated with any of these products and do not push any particular association or style of BJJ. This stuff works regardless of your Helio or Carlos following, which finally leads me to why this was written under a pseudonym.

As a practicing BJJ student and coach, my affiliation is with a certain association (try saying that when you've had a couple of shots). Some of the ideas outlined in this manual are very much contrary to what my association prescribes, and are frowned upon by my own professor and the association I am very much part of.

This has more to do with the political system in which these elements exist. Considering the culture that Brazilian Jiu Jitsu was born in: a crucible of brothers, fathers, mothers, politics and factions make it very difficult for the culture not to seep through into the art form.

The country in which I was born was very much a partisan place with deep-rooted attitudes from religion to which was your favorite football team. I personally feel that this type of thought process no longer belongs on the mat. You may feel different. All the protocols will still work although you may feel uncomfortable with a couple of them, more specifically, training at another academy that allows drop-in students. So as a sign of respect for my professors and teammates I will remain sincerely yours ... anonymous.

HOW TO USE THIS MANUAL

Pretty much however you like. If you have the paperback version you might like it so much that you use it to dip into on a regular basis as a reminder of the ideas. You might also hate it so much that you keep it handy in the bathroom in case of emergency. Either way I hope you give the theories due consideration. They are not carved in stone, I do not promote myself as any kind of expert or guru, these are just concepts that you can use and/or adapt for your own purposes. My only goal is only that you improve your game. End of sermon.

It is worth mentioning here that it is probably a good idea to read the book all the way through and then get the tools necessary to implement it (not necessary to have all of them but some of them will help for sure) and then start. Just do it.

It is also my recommendation that you begin on the first of the month and have a boxed calendar (I got a free one from a Chinese restaurant) posted on a wall somewhere visible. After every session - drilling, rolling or at the academy - put a large red 'X' through that date. As you see the X's build this will encourage you to continue, a bit like marathon runners mile markers. They show progress and the distance to the finish line.

It is my hope that when this work is done you will have a short break and take some time to reflect and then come back to this system again and again. Brazilian Jiu Jitsu once it's in your blood is hard to give up and hard to ignore.

Ask yourself this question: If you were offered a million dollars today and in exchange you would be stripped of your rank and all your skills, plus you would never be permitted to train in Jiu Jitsu or anything similar for the rest of your life, would you accept the million dollars?

The answer to this question will tell you more about your future BJJ journey than any other question I could have asked you.

CHAPTER ONE: WHITE BELT MINDSET

I'm an avid learner. This always puts me in a White Belt mindset even if I know a ton about a particular subject. Researching this book was a great experience for a review of the system I had developed and to get down and dirty into some of the nooks and crannies of each individual area. Not only did I find out what made such leaps and bounds in my BJJ game but I also delved deep enough to find out why.

EMPTY YOUR TEACUP

"Empty your mind, be formless, shapeless - like water. Now you put water into a cup, it becomes the cup, you put water into a bottle, it becomes the bottle, you put it in a teapot, it becomes the teapot. Now water can flow or it can crash. Be water, my friend."
~ Bruce Lee

Bruce got it right. You need to hit the mat (and just about every learning experience) as if it was the first time you ever rolled. It's a sad part of Jiu Jitsu and many martial arts that ego is a part of paying to play. There is always someone at the school that is a pain in the ass and wants to smash everyone on the mat. If they don't get a sub or two by the end of the session then they've had a bad roll.

This is sad. Just make sure it isn't you doing this.

Hurting your training partners is a bums game and very short sighted. If you've ever played around with a bunch of kids you don't smash pass them and then from side control, jump knee to stomach. Do you?

So why blast though a couple of white belts and feel great about it? This is just operating from a place of fear and insecurity.

When we step on the mat we need to be attentive to our professors and our coach. Don't bring preconceived notions or preconceived elements of yourself into the academy. You might be the next Roger Gracie but until you lift a few golds at the World Championships keep your pie-hole shut, your mind open and learn something.

This is also the mindset you need with this program. This is a thirty-day solution and working in private sessions and coaching at my school I have duplicated amazing results repeatedly using that timeline. When I coach a student one-on-one I ask for an empty mind, some ask 'Why? Shouldn't I know what I'm aiming to do?' It's good to be curious, and it is, but not right now.

Give up the ego and the mind for just thirty days and allow a transformation to take place. Be water, my friend.

LEARNING

In most coaching systems the adaptation or use of the four learning styles is usually mentioned. They were originally developed in an organized fashion by Noel Burch of the Gordon Training System in the seventies but have always been attributed to the social psychologist Abraham Maslow.

The Four Learning States provide a model for skill learning and that's a major element in studying any martial art. Starting with the unconscious competence phase. This is the 'we don't even know that we don't know much' stage of development and then the realization that we need to learn that skill. Think about your own very first steps onto the mat.

Eventually the skill can be brought about so that you understand that you don't know too much and finally you process that into a reflex action. This is the final stage called unconscious competence and probably what your professor displays. He will roll into a position he has been in so many times that the escape or submission is purely a reflexive action.

This process as outlined in the next section can help you develop blind spots that you miss and deal with your self awareness in the four stages. It's important that you are aware of your current state of development and then we will look at how three of these four apply to your BJJ progress.

THE FOUR STAGES

1. **Unconscious incompetence** The student does not understand or know how to do something and does not necessarily recognize the deficit. They may deny the usefulness of the skill. The individual must recognize their own incompetence, and the value of the new skill before moving on to the next stage. The length of time an individual spends in this stage depends on the strength of the stimulus to learn. The 'Why' of learning.

2. **Conscious incompetence** Though the individual does not understand or know how to do something, he or she does recognize the deficit, as well as the value of a new skill in addressing the deficit. The making of mistakes can be integral to the learning process at this stage.

3. **Conscious competence** The individual understands or knows how to do something. However, demonstrating the skill or knowledge requires concentration. It may be broken down into steps, and there is heavy conscious involvement in executing the new skill.

4. **Unconscious competence** The individual has had so much practice with a skill that it has become "second nature" and can be performed easily. As a result, the skill can be performed while executing another task. The individual may be able to teach it to others, depending upon how and when it was learned.

[1].Reference Wikipedia: ^ **a b c** "Conscious competence learning model matrix - unconscious incompetence to unconscious competence". Business Balls.

THE STAGES ADAPTED FOR JIU JITSU

Keep forgetting techniques? Not grappling as well as you should? Maybe you just don't know what you don't know as mentioned above in the first stage: 'unconscious incompetence'.

Below is an adaptation on how we apply the data above so that it makes sense in a Jiu Jitsu context or drilling session.

To win in a match or sparring session then you need to get from Point A (usually a standing or kneeling position) to Point B, this could be a submission or you could break things down further and consider a transition, sweep, pass or move to a dominant position as success. This seems straightforward but do you have the links clear in your mind that get you from A to B to C...?

I am going to use an adapted version of the four learning stages for our purposes in Jiu Jitsu. Ignoring the unconscious competence area, as you already know that some part of your game is lacking (or you are a white belt and have no real concept of the techniques yet), we move on to phase one:

1. The Cognitive Phase. This is the process where you see the parts of a technique. Consider the armbar. It takes several stages to get from the closed guard to the armbar as an example:

A. Secure the arm you want to attack
B. Place the foot on the hip
C. Swivel your own hips to create angle
D. Throw leg over face
E. Lift hips for tap

This is a (very) simplified version but you get the drift. Most beginners see this process and try to speed through it. This is a mistake. At the cognitive phase the opposite should be true. Slow down. Understand each step, when your professor or coach mentions a detail then concentrate on the detail, this will be important - I guarantee it. Make it slow enough that you understand how the pieces fit together.

This advice applies to all levels. When Marcelo Garcia samples some new position he doesn't just watch it on YouTube then start flying into it in the academy. He will study the chain of events that comprise the technique, link them together in his mind and then drill it possibly adding his own flavor (but he's a genius so don't do the flavor bit when you are drilling a new technique). Which leads us to:

2. The Associative Phase. This is where you can visualize yourself flowing through the entire technique. <u>WITH NO PARTS MISSING</u>. Once you know physically how the pieces fit together, stop and see in your mind how that process works. If you can visualize yourself moving through the whole process that means that you understand the technique. If you get brainfog or amnesia half way through, drill it again - slowly - in steps and realize which part you left out. Once you start rolling you can try the technique and if it doesn't come off check in and see what happened. This is covered in more depth in the section on Observation.

It's important to recognize that some people stop here. They learn the steps, they can see it in their minds, they sample it in sparring - it works. No need for further exploration. They are short changing themselves. They need to continue to:

3. The Autonomous Phase. This is where the stimulus automatically produces response. Let me offer a real world example. One of my favorite stances (starting positions) in sparring is the Butterfly Guard. So I sit with my knees splayed and am very conscious of the distance between my training partner and myself. I then hunt for the cross-collar and elbow grip, I can get this most times as it can be very non-threatening to my opponent. Once hooked in my partner only has a few options. I have drilled every possible option at least a hundred times each.

Doesn't matter to me if they grab my pants at the knee, below the knee, break my grip, posture up, scoot to the right, scoot to the left, or push their weight forward. I pretty much have a set piece response. Now this isn't to say that I cannot be passed or my partner won't have a counter to my attack but I do know that I don't have to think too much so that I can counter his counter if

15

necessary or worry more about the pass if it looks like he has broken my technique.

If an arm is presented I will have an attack for the arm. If my partner slips up in anyway I am pretty much prepared. This was a revelation to me. For the first couple of years I was just rolling around getting very sweaty and sore in the process. Then something clicked, this usually only happens after tons of reps and a roadmap of what I should be repping.

Think about it. If you learn to drive stick shift, you know: control the clutch, change gears with your hand, etc. You take stick shift driving test and pass. Congrats!

Then you put the car away and three years later think, let's take her for a spin. How do you imagine you would handle the controls? You might pull it off but you've dropped back to the Cognitive Phase. Nice and slow and going through the steps consciously hoping you don't stall it at a traffic signal on the highway.

Now if you've been driving stick for three years every day I bet sometimes you arrive at your destination and can't even remember the journey?? That's how automatic your sense of process has been. You are in phase four, the Autonomous Phase. No thought, just action. And this is where we want to (eventually) aim.

This is much harder to accomplish in the striking arts. For example, how many hooks does a boxer have to slip before it becomes reflex? Probably thousands, so we need to count our blessings that the gentle art does afford us some time to adapt. Things move at a much slower pace in grappling and this should make our drilling efforts much more efficient.

Ultimately it boils down to taking things one step at a time, or gradient learning. The mindset of 'gotta have it now' won't work with most proficiencies and Jiu Jitsu is no different. Get to a point where you can just complete the move or technique then set about drilling it.

A final note on 'drilling' or 'repping' a technique. Make sure you understand it and that all the various points are in place **before** you drill. A bodybuilder would not carry out thousands of reps on a body part that was already well developed. And you should not be repping a technique badly.

This is where your road map comes in. Stick to the plan. Rest when you need (or should) and keep moving forward when you are assigned to do so. Don't start straying off the path, the overall result will be less powerful.

CONFRONTATION

1. the act or an instance of confronting
2. a situation of mutual hostility between two powers or nations without open warfare
3. a state of conflict between two antagonistic forces, creeds, or ideas etc.

Pretty much everything you encounter on your Jiu Jitsu path will boil down to the ability to confront things or ideas. In fact, that's pretty much life in general. Your ability to confront the stages of gradient learning in the Jiu Jitsu process will have the greatest impact here.

When you are having a hard time learning a particular technique or just struggling in sparring etc. this is generally that you are lacking the ability to confront and engage that particular area.

For example: If I notice a student is tough at sparring and strong but does not think their game through then they will keep getting caught and submitted. The best thing to do with this student is to pull them back onto the learning path:

Plan out a series of attacks from start to completion. Slowly.

Get them to look at their opponents' habit patterns and strengths in their game. And then cover each step drilling the technique until they achieve a visible combination of toughness, strength plus good technique.

The ability to engage when your whole physiology and psychology is telling you otherwise is a huge part of breaking through levels in everything you do. Anything you are good at, anything you can do with a great proficiency is because you have the ability to engage it. And with a big smile on your face. Some students have a great natural ability and I enjoy tough rolls as much as the next man but tapping out is never easy. If I get tapped I always walk away from the academy and try to deconstruct the attack or position so that I can confront this situation with more confidence next time.

If you feel trepidation about a particular position, then you will need to confront and engage that position more frequently and when you start your map in the thirty-day protocol build that in at the beginning, when energy is the highest.

Break things back into steps. Say you are having trouble with side control top. Start with controlling your partners' hips. Get familiar hand positions (grips) that work well to keep the hips controlled. Add more pressure using shoulders or grips. Ask your professor where you start. But break it down. It makes the ability to confront and engage much easier than sparring with someone who you just can't hold down when you've passed into a great position.

This is how I deal with new students when I'm coaching. Thanks to the UFC and various MMA shows on TV new students come to Jiu Jitsu with a mixture of notions from a monastic retreat for people who like wearing Karate pajamas to a Brad Pitt style Fight Club. They start to see people roll and they tense up, stomachs knotting in the process. Everything is so close now, so real and they think they are up next for a good old choking session.

This is why it's best to start them off easy. Even if they want to just jump in and have a 'rassle'. We cover closed guard, distance, breaking the guard, a simple submission. Then we will drill for a while. If I feel comfortable I'll even introduce them to a short specific training session. Closed guard rotation, for example, but I tell them if they are in the guard their only objective is to break the guard, I don't even want them to pass yet.

After a while they are breaking, passing and moving into position. Suddenly the thing that made blood drain from their faces (or in some cases shot them into a bugged eyed frenzy) looks like they've been doing it quite a while. They are comfortable, and this is how you confront and engage the positions you are having trouble with: break everything down into steps (cognitive phase) then see yourself doing it (associative phase) then drill it until it's comfortable (autonomous phase).

Anything, and I mean anything, you are having trouble with, break it down into steps first. Then work on it until you feel comfortable. You'll be gaining ground in no time.

OBSERVATION

Any system of learning needs a method of recognition, or reflection. I often use the phrase with students 'Know where you are first'. This doesn't refer to the schools location and zip code. It means when someone has you in half guard top with an under-hook and head control, you should recognize this.

In any system of defense there has to be a recognition of the attack type, and I have found that many Jiu Jitsu schools are very vague on this point, asking the student to rely on their rolling intuition. Going back to the previous learning phases though, for the most part the student doesn't realize that he has to recognize what position his opponent is in. This seems crazy to me. Most students understand their own position: closed guard, deep half guard, butterfly, X-guard, etc. but what is happening to the organism on the other end of this transaction - your partner or opponent?

There is a definite instruction protocol for pretty much every aspect of teaching martial arts, with the exception of recognizing what your opponent seemed to be doing at every stage of training.

Until Dan Anderson (the famed American Freestyle Karate Instructor) developed what he calls 'Monitoring'. It applies to both attacking and defending, but the easiest way to understand it is via defense or transitioning from an unfavorable position to a better one, which is essential to improving your game. For the sake of this BJJ manual I will refer to this as 'Observation' or 'Knowing where you are' and 'What is happening.'

General Concept
Observation of your partner then is the effective ability to consciously be aware of opponents' movements as he begins to do them. Most students use strength to cover up this process. Grabbing onto your opponent as if your life depended on it isn't a long-term strategy for success. For the most part it will be seen as stalling and your gas tank will run dry before you even work out what's happening. By the same rule 'the scramble' is another

example. You're not sure what your opponent is doing (and neither do you) but if you keep moving then you might just recover and end up on your knees facing your opponent, well done, you've escaped. Neither of these are cognitive processes, they are knee-jerk reactions and this is what we need to stop.

Easier said than done.

Bottom line: The decision to confront and handle the position comes too late, this then leads to survival instincts: wild, dangerous, injurious and haphazard techniques developing.

When you use Observation you are **conscious** of your opponents movements at all times. You monitor all his attacking units (grips, foot position) as well as his balance (hips, knees, weight distribution). When Observing the attacking units you know where these are at all times, you can see them and then take action accordingly. These may change as you begin to observe again. It's like an internal Satellite Observation System.

You want to spot the way your opponent distributes his weight. This is his base-point. He will have some form of starting position (standing or kneeling) and you should be able to clearly see from his weight and stance where he will aim his attack. You can see this and intercept it by working your own game first, imposing your game. This throws Observation back to him. In short, there should be no surprises.

This is not easy. It requires being **awake** and **aware** of your opponent in every sparring session. As you progress, you should be able to monitor your opponent and then move him into a position that suits your game but makes him feel comfortable, or non-threatened. Most Jiu Jitsu practitioners are 70% asleep when they spar and I've come across plenty of 90 to 100% in total snooze mode. They are hardly aware of their own movements, just going through motions, never mind the positions I'm trying to impose. This is how the same technique or sucker move constantly catches the same training partners time after time.

When you generate a higher level of awareness of yourself and your opponent, you do not tend get suckered. Period. Concentrate by staying awake and speaking to yourself internally (he has a grip on my knee and my collar, his hips are high though, I can get the under-hook from here...) and you'll have this down pat in no time.

Technical Approach

It's worth mentioning that there are specific and general Observation conditions. General Observations are strength and size considerations. We've all heard the Helio stories of the art being developed for 'men with bodies like dead chickens' and this was cool when no one knew what BJJ was. These days, someone steps on the mat with a college wrestling background and muscles in his spit then you had better have a strategy to consider. What if your sparring partner is three hundred pounds? You can see from a general Observation standpoint that you do not want to be on bottom ... unless you're four fifty in which case - you da man!

You cannot get grips unless you lean forward or extend your arms. You cannot launch on top without the use of the legs. These are general trigger points that you should be aware of.

If you are starting on your knees, imagine a line drawn on the mat between you and your opponent horizontally, like you are sat in front of a mirror. If either you or your opponent can cross this line and you can reach (touch) each other. Then this is the critical distance line (CDL). This is the area of no mans land which tells you a lot about general Observation. You should be able to devise your strategy from here, as soon as a hand or foot crosses that line you need to know what the next move will be ... **regardless of whose hand or foot crosses that line**.

Specific Observations are the understanding of the attacking units themselves, namely: grips, foot position (which develops the stance). This is where 95% of your concentration should be focused. If you mentally divide your opponents body down the center as soon as he takes his stance and you monitor his hands he will either get a grip closer to himself (on a pant leg or the collar closest to him) he may go deeper and come for a deep collar or sleeve grip then he will move the second hand. The exception to this would be simultaneous grips, which is rare as most practitioners prefer to get a sense of balance or create tension before latching the next grip.

Each attack will have three parts (1) grips, (2) transition, and (3) position. You want to change the path of the attack at the second phase the transition. This is the easiest way to counter. If you need to change your strategy or have more time - release (break) the grips - no one attacks without some form of grip. If you are attacking first then you will work your protocol, but the process will more than likely be the same: grips, transition, position (and if you've drilled it well enough), submission.

You will need to intercept their transition at the beginning of the phase - certainly not at the end. This can lead to your guard being passed and then you will need another counter. To do this you will need to (a) monitor the baseline of your opponent closely so you can see which side his weight shifts, and (b) install your strategy as soon as he begins his attack. These you can drill once you get into the thirty-day program.

Most students don't even think about the counter until the attack is well on its way. This is a folly. They sleep through the grips and foot position and don't even realize that an attack is happening until they land in side control or a scramble. Proper Observation and good execution and grip control should cut this down quite a bit.

To make Observation even easier to work with, use the technique known as 'side-tracking'. You form a grip structure or stance you are happy with. Until you get the grips you want break your opponents grips all the time. You then assign a technique that covers any position if your opponent moves to the left, you have a left side counter. If he moves to the right then you have a right side counter (from the stance and grips you have). If he breaks your grip, you have a counter and if he leans backward or forward you have attacks.

There are four positional strategies you would need to learn: left side, right side, grip break, leaning (forward or backward). There should be no crossover techniques. This will expose quickly if you are awake or not.

I drilled this for a couple of weeks then found that when my opponent moved right I did the left hand technique and was handily passed because I confused myself by being asleep and not drilling enough. It didn't matter though. The fact that I thought about it, saw the move coming and had a strategy made me feel pretty good. Another week later and no one passed the stance I was starting with and I was moving into great positions time after time. The drilling side of things in steps worked wonders.

Most students' positions are less than spectacular usually because (1) they went into full on sparring too soon, (2) they have been taught only technique positions and are unaware of transitions, (3) they have not been taught how to spot an attacking grip, and/or (4) they have failed to confront and engage the attack.

Number (4) is the most common.

Now you have a method for creating awareness, spotting an attack and countering. Enough practice and these should become natural movements. Now it just needs the accompanying physical work and the rest will follow.

Recap: Creating awareness while sparring, you have to, in this order:
1. Monitor the attacking units. Concentrate and focus. Mentally move forward with the attack until you recognize what your opponent plans to do. Reaching out and crossing the critical distance line means you are ready to confront and engage your opponent.
2. Spot the attack and counter the transition as soon as it begins
3. Counter and move into a position of control
4. Counter failed, break grips and reset

Focus intently on the hips at all times, as this is the balance of power and know **at all times** where your own hips are.

If you are having trouble and still getting suckered from time to time then try this. Observe the attacking units 100% even your own when attacking. You will still need to move and pass or submit but keep these areas in your periphery. It's a little weird at first as we are so intent on reaching our target but a few things can happen.

When you are intently focused on hands and feet of your opponent you are better prepared for counter attacks. After a while just focus on hands and your own hips, you'll find adjustments in range and pressure easier to handle. The strange phenomenon with this technique is that it helps tremendously with passing the guard, just keep the pass in the periphery and stay focused on the hands, feet and hips and you'll just slip by your opponent.

Principles

You have a sensory radius around your body that is constantly on alert. We like to think of this as our 'personal space'. Someone gets too close in the line at Starbucks and we get that uncomfortable feeling. Something or someone can only get to a certain distance before it enters into your Observation Sphere.

The main principle behind Observation is to expand that personal space so that it includes your opponent. He twitches and you feel it. Your opponents' very presence warrants Observation.

Phase two of this process is to feel fine about him being in your space. It's strange that you need to get even more personal when you're involved in a martial art that involves sweaty wrestling. Total acceptance of this opponent in your space will make you more relaxed where as resistance can only make you more nervous and rigid.

The calming effect makes your overall perception even greater: the world seems to expand. Please don't confuse calm with laziness; this will only get you submitted quicker. The essence of calm is being devoid of nervous constricting tension while staying on full alert. Be aware but not frozen by the actions of your opponent, you will be amazed by what you can feel and see when you reach this level of relaxed alert condition.

Combine this technique with the mechanics of the thirty-day program and you will have the entire ethos for Jiu Jitsu success.

CHAPTER TWO: A 30 DAY PROTOCOL

THE PROCESS: IN A NUTSHELL.

Putting the protocol together in a nutshell:

- Develop a plan that concentrates on one position for the next 30 days
- You will train in BJJ (a lesson in the academy or drilling at home) for one hour minimum every day for 30 days
- On drilling sessions you will follow one position only
- You will record each session in a journal or Jiu Jitsu Log
- Before every lesson or drilling session you will review your Log
- In every sparring session you will practice the techniques you have drilled
- At the end of the 30 days you will rest for four days.

And that's it. Simple right? Let's break those ideas apart and look at some tools that will help with the process.

THE IDEA BEHIND THE IDEA

The successful entrepreneur Benny Lewis, the guy behind the *Fluent in 3 Months* program, put it much better than me. He has a story of his own and this was how his business was formed.

Benny, an Irish Engineering student, ended up stationed in Spain after his graduation. This was a dream position for him but he couldn't speak Spanish. He thought he would arrive on the job and then learn it as he went along. This became increasingly frustrating for him, not that he couldn't communicate, as it turned out most of his dealings were with British people or well-meaning English speaking Spaniards, but his linguistics did not improve as he expected.

Six months into his new position he was disappointed that he still could not speak Spanish well. He set himself a task; he would only speak Spanish (even in it's rudimentary form) for the next thirty days - no exceptions. Thirty days can't hurt.

At first it was a little embarrassing as lots of hand signals were required to get his point across, but it also created an amazing side effect: You pick up another language extremely quick if you don't have your native language to fall back on. Within even a few short weeks he was speaking the language comfortably. The one-month immersion was far more effective than the previous six months of just giving it a try. He was impressed with progress but now he really wanted to see if this could work with other languages. He moved to Berlin, learned German, moved to France learned French and then really went for it - moved to Prague and learned Czech, which is an extremely difficult language to learn.

He then put his career on hiatus and traveled the world; within two years he could speak seven languages fluently. The method worked. Language hacking was born.

We can apply similar principles to Brazilian Jiu Jitsu. It's technical and uses leverage to produce a result. Why not use an immersion system for thirty days that works to produce amazing results. What do you say...fluent in BJJ in thirty days!

Like Benny though there has to be a commitment - 30 days, no exceptions. The work will be tough and unyielding but if you can put partying or family on the back burner (or use a workaround, there is a chapter on Workarounds) then the results can be nothing short of spectacular.

Can you commit to thirty days? That's the only homework you'll have from this section: Finding that commitment.

THE MAP

You will need an objective; a goal to reach during the next 30 days or you'll feel lost.

Getting lost? You need a map. Not necessarily a physical map but a list of positions that you will want to drill and become comfortable with.

It's beyond the scope of this short manual to layout hundreds (if not thousands) of plans as a lot has to do with your stage of development. This is covered in more detail in the next section 'Progression'.

So how do you develop a personalized map in the first place? You need to start at the place you least want to start at (remember confront and engage), which is your weakest position. Only you will know this. For a lot of starting students side-control-bottom and mount-top cause them a lot of problems. This is usually compounded when a higher-ranking student mauls you in one of these positions.

It's not unusual to go through the fundamental curriculum in around three to four months depending on your school. This involves self defense techniques as well as foundational Jiu Jitsu instruction and you may have been sparring or doing some specific training at this time.

Which position makes you uncomfortable? Go there first that's where the gold is. Can't submit anyone? Go there first. It is also my recommendation that if you are going to focus on submissions then work to move to the back and sub from there.

Some recent data has been compiled due to the amazing efforts of Tyler Bishop at BishopBjj.com and the most effective submission area, as of the 2012 world championships, is the submission from the back. It's a dominant position and a good place to start with submission drills.

Whatever frustrates you on the mat decide to master that area in the next thirty days.

For example, if side control bottom is a weak point then you will use that as your focus. I can almost here the taunts from the back of the room. There's not a lot to side control bottom ... How do I drill that for 30 days? I'll be bored senseless!! That's where the list comes in. Let's break it backward:

1. Side control (SC) bottom when opponent has head and arm control (headlock version)
2. Standard side control bottom when opponent has head and hip blocked.
3. Standard SC Bottom with head and arm blocked
4. SC Bottom when opponent flattens the hip shield (sea shell)
5. SC Bottom when opponent moves north/south
6. SC Bottom ...

The positions and variables are almost infinite. Write a list, maybe use a BJJ Book or website. A good source of technical data is the BJJ Technique Catalog by Dave Thomas and is available for the crazy price of 'free' (as of this writing) online at http://bjjtech.com/tech/

If you want to pay for a similar service but with a more comprehensive video representation of each technique you might want to consider Bob Dorris' excellent BJJ Database known as iGrapple (http://www.igrapple.com)

Once you have a list, you have a plan of attack. Move the most difficult position you are having trouble with to the top of the list - remember energy is highest at the beginning. This is technique one, then the next, that's two and so on.

If you want more submissions, then you need to follow the principle: position, transition then submission. Concentrate on getting to a position that you can submit your opponent from, like the back.

Let's come back to side control again by way of example. Let's say you would like to be effective in subbing an opponent from side control. The map might look something like this.

- Move to half guard
- Old School Sweep to side control
- Fake knee on belly
- Switch to Kimura, or baseball choke, or ... you get the idea.

You can see this begins with step one of the gradient learning process outlined in the previous chapter. Let's break it down some more. Step one was - move to half guard.

Research the various entry methods to half guard, where it acts as a guard and has the options of sweeping or maybe uses the knee shield. It would be a good idea to review half guard with head controlled, half guard with under-hook, and deep half guard. You have a short list, it could be a lot longer if you really delve into the half guard. Caio Terra demonstrates 111 half guard variations in his DVD set and I'm sure that's just the tip of the iceberg.

Bolt onto this: half guard sweeps from standard half guard and deep half guard, especially the ones where you finish in side control.

Look into three submissions from side control. You will more than likely have to feign one attack forcing your opponent to defend then apply an attack of your own. All of these techniques can be found in some really good books that are readily available and pretty much every variation of every BJJ technique is now on YouTube so you can review the ideas there too.

Ask your Professor or coaches for ideas based on what you are trying to do IN EACH STAGE. Don't just research the sub, you have to work the entry, move to the position then the submission. There are no shortcuts. Sure, there are some fancy moves that come off, but leave that to the other guy while you work to becoming consistently spectacular.

Write the map down. My map now consists of 112 techniques right now. I drill the ones I'm working on then rediscover the first few so I don't get sloppy. It takes me an hour or so to drill four or five techniques effectively and every time I review the details before I drill. We'll cover this more in the section on Drilling.

PROGRESSION

In the excellent book 'Jiu Jitsu University', by Saulo Ribeiro with Kevin Howell, they describe the progress of a student through the belts by demonstrating the phases a student should develop. This is an interesting concept and one that I actually believe works. When developing your map you may want to consider these stages as your phase of development and concentrate on that particular area.

- White Belt - Survival
- Blue Belt - Escapes
- Purple Belt - Guard
- Brown Belt - Guard Passing
- Black Belt - Submissions

This is quite an interesting path to take and shows a clear route to Black Belt. Don't be too rigid and think, I'm a Blue Belt so I can only work on escapes. That's not true. As I outlined in the previous section there are so many individual paths to follow that there are no hard and fast rules.

This is just a concept, a guide. If you want to put a map together and feel that you aren't sure of any real holes in your game right now then I would suggest playing up to the next level. If you are Blue then put a map together based on creating an effective guard you to feel comfortable playing from.

Bottom line you need to have the ability to draw a line from point A to point B. If you fail to plan, you plan to fail.

ORIENTATION

When armies march they need good map-readers, or they tend to get lost. These map-readers and route leaders they follow are usually members of the Signals Regiment. This is the team that puts the signals in position ahead or they have small units to lead the signal and these are called Orienteers.

It's amazing that orienteering is now a leisure pursuit of it's own. Teams are given ordnance maps and coordinates to various zones plus a compass and that's it, whoever gets to the final destination point (the focus goal) first wins. Pretty simple. But without the map and compass it's almost impossible, especially over very long distances.

This particular section isn't just about the map of techniques that you are following but about the orientation of your sparring - when you get to that stage.

A lot of mistakes and confusion in sparring comes from lack of orientation. As an example, have you ever noticed how much easier a roll becomes when you decide on a single approach to the session. You say, I'm going to work my half guard sweep, and bam everything revolves around it and it works for the most part. But if you just roll then you just have a great workout because it was harder to attack. If you have a position of focus (an orientation) you automatically reduce the number of options you present to your training partner (and yourself) so the roll in its essence becomes simpler.

If we look at the orientation as a filter then all techniques have to pass through that position and it narrows all other techniques. Just like the filter on the lens of a camera, if the filter is set to blue then everything the camera sees if varying shades of blue. A small blob of orange doesn't just pop up in a photo, it cannot, as it is filtered away with all the other frequencies in the spectrum.

With orientation you work with one orientation filter until you feel good with it, then you move on to the next one.

When you are starting out it is good to get a handle on orientation filters because it gives you some sense of direction. Your map should contain at least one of these orientation filters, and should be an ideal position you feel comfortable to operate from.

If you are a white belt consider the closed guard attacks and defenses as a good orientation filter. This is a good position to present and receive feedback. As you grow and learn more techniques at the academy you have to give up the more comfortable orientation filters, if you feel safe in a particular orientation filter (like the closed guard) then it's time to move to a new one. There are no Jiu Jitsu champions (or black belts) who are just good at closed guard and have low-grade open guards.

Once you feel safe, move onto the next, then when you are sparring move forwards and backwards between the orientation modes.

Most BJJ students don't work this way. They don't have several operational filters and get stuck in one or two. The problem with this approach is that most of your opponents are different: body shapes, weights, experience levels, etc. You must have room to adapt.

If you are aware that the only reason you are staying in one operational filter is that you feel safe. This in essence is just fear of the tap that stops you experimenting with a new filter. We have a guy at our academy who has a killer guillotine and another with a killer triangle. This is great for the team as it keeps our guillotine and triangle defenses real sharp. Once you defend these two techniques though against these guys, they've really got nothing else to offer, they just fall apart, get passed then flop about trying to recover and usually get subbed. They are both gold medalists though, so having killer submissions is essential, but becoming a fully rounded black belt? Both these guys are way off the pace.

Get good at one guard, or one submission then move on. This doesn't mean that you are no longer allowed to use that approach but try something new. Have a new starting focus, a new orientation filter. Pull the killer moves out from under the bed every so often, dust them off and treat someone to a tap out, just don't get stuck into thinking this your only option.

I used to hate side control top. For some reason I could not get good control or an acceptable submission. My Map changed to this: use my killer A-Sweep to get them on their back, instead of going for the back or the mount, I would pull back and fall into side control. This forced me to work on the new orientation filter I was drilling. At first it was frustrating as my mount submissions felt great and really worked, I got a real handle on the Roger Gracie cross collar choke from the mount, but I didn't go safe, I pushed into territory that exhausted me and made me feel lame.

Then something weird happened. My orientation filter fell into place. All the details were there, with a couple of slight adjustments my opponent fell right into place and a kimura fell right into my hands ... with virtually no effort. Okay. It's worked one time.

I went again, it worked again, little more effort than last time but it came off, then I got my groove on and it became pretty consistent. Black belts defended it well, but by then I was working on transition from that orientation filter so the sparring sessions just went on and on ... with me on the attack and my team mates with something to think about.

Aside from guard positions you can also work other orientation filters. Work a specific sub, as in the example above, work your transitions, work your balance and posting, work your Observation, work your breathing ... there are a lot of options for orientation filters.

On a slow night, I like to move through three or four mode changes so I can tell if I'm getting rusty in a particular technique/guard. But I am aware of the operational modes I am changing through.

The best way to start with an operational filter is to "have a great guard" a Go-To Guard. I will never forget my Professor telling us all in class (and this was an advanced Black Belt class) that our guards all stank! Literally, just like that "Your guards suck!" He wasn't playing around and he didn't call out any individuals but as far as I was concerned he was talking to me.

At home later, I went back to the drawing board. Read all I could on guards, watched the videos and placed a notice in the garage near my mats - Guard! Then drilled a lot of guard game and passes. These days I have a pretty good open and closed guard. There's no magic, it was my orientation filter, I had a map and I knew where I was going. Did my guard get passed? Sure, but nowhere near as often until none of the other guys the same rank as me could pass. It was pretty solid. The side effect, it's easier to spar and roll when your guard is tough to pass and it also gave me time to think and work my game.

One of the main reasons starting with a good guard is important is because most of your partners will have a couple of good guard passes, then they might fall asleep if they don't get it. They didn't approach the roll with an orientation filter; they just wanted to pass your guard. It's automatic, and when it doesn't work they get frustrated, try something they are ill equipped to attempt and then get swept.

When you set up your guard you are doing so through an orientation filter, you await the pass then attack, or go straight into the attack if there is no pass coming. Most important of all though, it keeps you awake, keeps you focused.

Don't forget to sample different guards. Different strokes for different folks. You need the most appropriate guard for the most appropriate opponent. If you face off with Big Dave at the academy and he's three hundred pounds, use your head; closed guard is probably not an option because you can't close your guard unless you are six feet six with ultra long legs?? You are going to need some open and half guard options in play before you feel safe and complete.

DRILLING

drill [dril]
noun
1. Machinery, Building Trade.
a. a shaft-like tool with two or more cutting edges for making holes in firm materials, especially by rotation.
b. a tool, especially a hand tool, for holding and operating such a tool.

2. Military .
a. training in formal marching or other precise military or naval movements.
b. an exercise in such training: gun drill.

3. Any strict, methodical, repetitive, or mechanical training, instruction, or exercise: a spelling drill.

The effective use of drilling cannot be underestimated in this program. In fact, I would go as far as to say that if you took only one thing away from this manual it was this: Drill Everything.

In the bestselling book 'Outliers' Malcolm Gladwell points us to research that proves without doubt that practice time is the defining factor between most athletes and artists. The psychologists in the book were trying to debate if talent existed, the findings were amazing and the bottom line was talent or no talent, the artist or athlete that put in the most practice time ended up becoming the most talented.

"The emerging picture from such studies is that ten thousand hours of practice is required to achieve the level of mastery associated with being a world class expert - in anything," writes the neurologist Daniel Levitin. "In study after study, of composers, basketball players, fiction writers, ice skaters, concert pianists, chess players, master criminals, and what have you, this number comes up again and again. Of course, this doesn't address why some people get more out of their practice sessions than others do. But no one has yet found a case in which true world class expertise was accomplished in less time. It seems that it takes the brain this long to assimilate all that it needs to know to achieve true mastery."

10,000 HOURS OF PRACTICE.

Let's break it down (you'll have gathered that I like breaking things down to simple steps by now). That's 416 days in full 24 hours stages, but if we only train three times per week for one hour per session, that's 3,333 days to achieve excellence. That's nine years. Let's round it up and say to become a proficient Black Belt and you train consistently three times per week on average then it will probably take ten years to reach your goal. This is according to the 10K rule, which I agree with wholeheartedly. Read the book, the evidence is overwhelming.

To shorten this period of time to world class, the easiest way is to take this data on face value and apply it. Train six days per week. Drill three and train three (or more if you like). The drills you carry out should be no shorter than one hour, your training sessions should be a mixture of advanced and fundamental. Training with lower ranking players helps consolidate your progress and gives your body a rest ... but it's an hour on the clock - no excuses.

DO THIS AND YOU CAN BE WORLD CLASS IN ONLY 4.5 YEARS.

Drilling consists of repeating a chosen technique in perfect form for fifty repetitions. That's a workout, believe me. Break it down into two sets of twenty with a final set of ten. You can drill more but change the technique after the fifty are complete.

Before you drill, review your log (see the section on Recording), and concentrate on the task at hand. It's easy to go off track especially if the Internet is handy and you are drilling something from YouTube. It's an informative tool, don't get lost looking up cool flying triangles or Berimbolo sweeps (unless that's what you are planning to drill.)

This falls into the Attendance corner of the three A's triangle from the introduction. You have to show up to get better, that's true, but showing up and doing the right stuff can make a huge difference.

Don't take my word for it. Here are a couple of quotes from people who are training and winning:

"I drill techniques - my main techniques, my A-move, my A-game sweep, the guard pass and sub I hit the most, over and over again." This is from Keenan Cornelius, the purple belt (now brown belt) phenomenon to win every title he attempted in 2012. He continued, "I've drilled them so many times, my body just reacts now. I can go out and let instinct take over. Most of our training [at Lloyd Irvin] is drilling based on our individual games, and this is what we do best. Before a big tournament I stick to the stuff I've been doing and drill it to death. I used to try and think too much in the past. My master Lloyd [Irvin], told me that's a weakness. If you're thinking what to do next, your opponent is already moving to his next move. It's best to just react and let your body take over."

Obviously Keenan has moved from the Associative Phase of learning to the Autonomous Phase. His body has taken over and this has a massive impact on his composure in tournaments. His haul of gold in 2012 has been nothing short of miraculous. He looks to be a future champion to watch.

"Rolling is the only way to get good at Jiu Jitsu is a myth!" So says Rafael Lovato Jnr in his excellent course on Pressure Passing. "Rolling is a lot of FUN! And you should never stop rolling, but drilling is an AWESOME way to tighten up your game. So make sure you are rolling AND drilling together ... because this combo will take your game to another level when you really focus on both these things."

Beating a dead horse here but <u>drilling is KEY</u>. Most BJJ studios don't allow enough time (if any at all) to drill the techniques that are successful. There is a telling truth in a lot of the research regarding drilling, and that is "Play to your Strengths". Let's recap for a second: the map is a series of techniques that you plan to drill, and the map has been developed to introduce new skills or work on escapes from positions you are having trouble with. This is all valid. When you come to the drilling session though by way of warm up you can take two options or preferably employ both:

1. Have a light flow drill with a partner. This could be in the form of a light roll where neither of you stop in any position; just keep moving for five minutes straight. When you move to a position allow your partner to escape and maybe get into a better position, then you escape and move ... you do this for five minutes and you should be nice and loose.

2. Drill your favorite move for fifty repetitions. Personally I do two, I recover half guard to full guard, both sides for fifty reps. Then I drill closed guard to triangle for fifty reps, this is a great Ab workout. Does this improve my ability to recover from half guard and trap triangles from lots of different angles? What do you think?

The Pareto principle (80/20 rule) tells us that eighty percent of our results come from twenty percent of our efforts and we can lay this principle over most activities. This doesn't really prove much but one thing that has become evident over time is that most of our efforts in life are not distributed evenly in terms of outcome. Sometimes we can work really hard on something and receive very little recognition; sometimes we can hardly put in any input and come out smelling of roses.

Applying this concept to your BJJ Drilling. Let's say you have a killer armbar-triangle combo. For the first five minutes you will include this as your warm up. It's your A-game sub - this will be the first part of the system to fall into the Autonomous Phase. You will become so effective at the armbar-triangle that you will find you slap this on opponents or training partners without thinking. This is important for creating that groove in your brain that allows techniques to drop in automatically.

Don't think you just have to drill your weakest parts because you will find that as you improve you won't need to drill them, and this is a fundamental mistake. You need to drill your entire arsenal all the time. When you roll then you can try some new risky move, if it doesn't come off, you roll into a position you feel safe, then whap! you hammer home the killer move that you were pretty good at but now have gone on instinct. This is where the art comes into martial art. It's a sublime meditation and BJJ Nirvana.

NOTE: Do not go <u>hard</u> for the next thirty days. You will see in future sections that this is also a myth. Train smarter, not harder. And as another side note when I say 'hard' I am referring to full on sparring at 100% capacity. Hard as opposed to light rolling. It's important that you have full-on rolling in the next thirty days, you need to be challenged but not <u>every</u> time you roll.

CIRCUIT PATTERNS

Another thing with drilling you need to be aware of is the Circuit Pattern. A circuit is an automated response, one that happens that you are not aware of. This is the ideal we are searching for as described in the Autonomous phase, but what if your circuit patterns put you in a worse position!

The amount of awareness (or lack of) varies from position to position and in intensity of awareness. A circuit in electronics creates a pattern of moving electricity from one place to another in a repeatable manner - until the circuit breaks it will not vary from its path. And this is the same for habit patterns good or bad.

Let's say your brain is like a computer CPU circuit board.

When you are in the white belt phase you think about each position and learn them, as per Phase One of the learning cycle. Put a grip here, place your weight there, your partner gets away - oops! Forgot to block his hip, reset.

You go back and correct constantly giving the computer circuit feedback with what to do next and what not to do again. Then, as your skills improve and you move into the blue belt phase there is less conscious effort to learn the techniques. You have probably moved into the Advanced classes and gone beyond the fundamentals, sparring is easier and you have more of a handle on your own game and positions you prefer. This is a very delicate part of your development as this is where the position circuits begin to form. A solid circuit pattern is usually linked to emotion.

As soon as you feel elated that a particular sweep worked then the circuit locks down further, this happens more and more with each feeling of accomplishment. As you rely on each position to attack or counter there is a tendency to start applying this technique in most situations, especially emergency positions - instead of the more appropriate techniques that should be applied to that situation. You then start to fit the positions you have had success with into various guards and scrambles ... even when it's not the right technique in that position and clearly won't work? You can't stop yourself.

Let's say you get a great sweep to mount with the pendulum (or flower sweep) from closed guard and you score a lot with it. Each time you have 'success' this is lodged into the computer circuit 'score card'. The more plus deposits on the score card with the technique the more you use it. The more you use it the more muscle memory gets involved and the autonomous phase ingrains itself into the circuit pattern. It is now becoming more natural, more automatic. When the technique is fully embedded on automatic it scores itself and gets double plus points into the 'score card' column. And this is when you start to get stuck. You have now stored a _fact_ in your brain: This technique will work all the time on automatic and until the circuit is broken the computation will not be changed.

This also happens when a technique or position comes to you naturally or is easy to do. Students tend to be lazy when this occurs and whenever they get in a tight spot they fall back to this position or technique as a way of just defending or attacking without awareness.

This also means that many techniques and positions have not passed from the Cognitive Phase to the Associative Phase - this is due mainly to lack of drilling or practice. And usually they are not practiced or drilled because they can be difficult or complex to achieve. There is something wrong with this picture!

When you transition through a position into another position or submission attempt without awareness, without any thought for the pattern then that is a formed circuit. If it was the appropriate response for that situation and you were successful then give yourself a pat on the back, but if you were operating in a position and just went automatically to your Go-To move and it failed then this is a destructive circuit.

The way to overcome destructive circuits is first to become consciously aware of them, then also be aware of when you fall into the circuit. Then you can consciously work to break it. If you use your Go-To move and it fails then you have discovered a negative circuit, this is a great starting point for your map. Look for options when you get into this position and drill them as alternatives to your circuit.

What positions do you like best? What submissions come easiest to you? Which guard positions do you use the most? These are the first places to look for negative circuits.

When you discover a negative circuit, you'll know. You will feel bad that a technique you have success with didn't come off. It will amaze you that this technique just did not work. Ask your training partner why it didn't work and he'll tell you how he countered it - this is a negative circuit pattern beginning to form. Don't throw it away, take the technique to your coach or Professor and demonstrate what happened. They will usually point out some details you missed, it usually something that happened at the beginning of the technique and you might need to trace it all the way back. You will then need to drill this new technique ... it is not the same as the old one that came easy. Break its components down.

The hardest negative circuits to break are the ones that work really, really well.

Circuits can be found everywhere in your sparring sessions: positions, submissions, guards, sweeps - they are everywhere. Watch your opponents and training partners for patterns and then check yourself out. It's a base human condition.

You may be questioning this section, "But you said get to the auto-pilot phase! Isn't it best to just have an 'instinctive reaction'?"

Until you are very well accomplished then 'No'. You need to be aware of your body position and your opponents position at all times. The circuits I'm describing here are based upon lazy Jiu Jitsu and a more effective technique or position might have been a better option. Your Go-To techniques can be a lifesaver or they can just blow up at the wrong time, which makes your A-move pretty much useless and leaves you with no further options. No options is no good, trust me.

Don't make excuses for sleeping through a rolling session. It's better to be awake and engaged.

THE TRAINING DUMMY

What if you don't have an academy to train at? What if you train at a school but it's hard to make it every night of the week without divorce papers being filed? The easiest and in my opinion one of the most effective ways to drill is with a training dummy.

Training without a partner is still an excellent way to train. It's virtually impossible to train and have your partner available at all times, plus with a dummy your injury rate reduces dramatically. You can rep techniques and drill your A-moves concentrating on all the small details that make the difference. Even if you only have five or ten minutes spare, with a dummy you can drill for a short time and still feel an improvement.

There are many training dummies out there and I am not going to favor one over the other as I have not trained with them all. It's important that you can train effectively with a dummy and you can afford it. This is the criterion I used when selecting my own:

- Needs to be able to sit up so that closed guard drills work: armbars, omoplatas, triangles, etc.
- Keeps its legs up as a guard defense to practice guard passes.
- Returns its arms back to position so that you don't have to reset it after every rep.
- Keeps its posture in turtle position to practice back techniques, north/south and spinning to the back.
- Has a reasonable weight-ratio to simulate a real opponent. Too light doesn't work too well.
- Knees are positioned up so that stacking drills still work.

My dummy is so important to me that if I moved from one country to another I would make sure that I imported 'Burt' (that's what I call my dummy) with me. My personal choice was the Submission Master. This is not an inexpensive purchase but I believe it is the best of the submission dummies I tested and it met the entire criterion mentioned above.

You may think that a submission dummy is a huge investment and it's true that most dummies are not cheap, but when I compare Jiu Jitsu to most sports it's a pretty reasonable expense. Think about it, if you wanted to be a really good cyclist - the cost of a good bike? Say you wanted to be good at tennis or golf. Even if we take equipment off the table (which in golf terms is substantial) then the dues at the local tennis or golf clubs would make most BJJ players burst into tears. We get a great service from our academies for a pretty reasonable cost, adding to your tool kit is just a wise choice. I guarantee it.

The only time I see buying a dummy to be a waste is if it never gets used. Make sure when you decide to get a serious drilling aid like this that you build into your program time to drill with the dummy. What you should do is aim for one night per week (at least) when the academy has a time that doesn't suit your schedule and add that night in for 'Burt' night.

Take you laptop or iPad into the garage, lounge or wherever you store him and drill those techniques you've been struggling with. Keep the drilling format the same - the first five minutes should be your A-game submission or sweep and then when you're warm start using the visuals on YouTube, iPad or videos to practice. Not many real training partners will be this accommodating? ... Burt will.

When I first started using a dummy and drilling as I've described above I was accused of all kinds of nefarious activities it helped so much. I kept Burt under wraps mainly due to being self-conscious than anything else, I didn't want the guys to know I had a dummy or own up to using one. I'm pretty sure it would have been easier to admit taking steroids - which was one of the many accusations for the rapid improvement in technique.

My game literally went from zero to hero using the dummy and staying with the thirty-day program. At this time the thirty day program was just an idea and I had not formulated it as a system or measured its effectiveness. The dummy still paid off though as I started to make ground on good guys who I was always level with or slightly worse than. It's just 'Jiu Jitsu with Dummies'.

Can you imagine a boxer training without a heavy bag? What if a boxer turned to his coach and said, 'Sorry boss, not hitting the heavy bag tonight, seems like it might give me an advantage over my opponent.' Sure you'll agree this boxer sounds a bit punchy? So why do we look down on grappling dummies so much. I think this ties back to drilling. We never drill enough even though all the evidence points to the fact that drilling creates champions. The problem is that rolling is just a ton of fun. There is no getting away from the fact that Jiu Jitsu provides such a fun process of improvement due to the sparring aspect of the overall sport.

Still, boxers spar, boxers hit the bag and speedball because if they spent all their time sparring then they would be wondering where they were and what day it was by the time they hit their forties. Jiu Jitsu is much more forgiving in this aspect, so we roll, but that's not where the gold is. We need to drill effectively with or without a partner. No one bats an eyelid that we use training aids in the strength and conditioning portion of our training? Why not keep your game sharp using BJJ training aids? Let the gym membership go for a couple of months and grab a more productive tool.

As a warning make sure you don't purchase a throwing dummy thinking it will do the job and it's cheaper than its counterpart. Chances are it won't do the job at all (don't try to knock nails in wood with a pair of pliers, that's the wrong tool for the job) and you will have thrown your money down the drain. Your dummy needs to be Gi friendly and fit the bill outlined at the beginning of this section. When I say Gi friendly I mean a Gi needs to fit onto it so that you can still practice your grips. If you are more tenth planet than Nova Uniao then don't worry about the Gi so much but still make sure a rash-guard or tee-shirt will fit your dummy. Nothing worse than sweating all over a four hundred dollar investment and finding out there's no way to clean it! They tend not to fit in washing machines.

A grappling dummy is an excellent aid to your development. There is no other method of training - human or otherwise that can let you hit one hundred techniques in fifteen minutes. And you can include that as a cardio workout!

FAQ's from Submission Master on a Grappling Dummy by Bob Dorris

As you know, Bob sells the Submission Master grappling dummy. This is the dummy that I have but I have no affiliation to Bob or his organization and receive no commission or remuneration in any way for discussing his products. Please check different dummies out for yourself something new might be on the market that is just as effective.

Read what Bob has to say though, he knows his stuff on the training aid front, over to you Bob:

I'm always getting questions from readers about grappling dummy training, so I thought I'd share the Top 4 most frequently asked questions and my responses here with you.

1. What's the purpose of a grappling dummy?
2. Why train with a grappling dummy at all? Why not just use a live partner?
3. Is training "in class" enough?

FAQ #1: What's the purpose of a grappling dummy?

For getting HIGH REPETITIONS WITHOUT A PARTNER. That's it. End of story. Repetitions create muscle memory. Muscle memory allows you to complete movements (techniques) quickly and in a coordinated way without having to consciously think about the action. Of all the things you can do to improve your skill, creating muscle memory is undoubtedly the #1 thing you should focus on.

I like to say repetitions are like "rolling a marble through the dirt..." The more times you roll the marble the same way, the deeper the groove in the dirt becomes and the EASIER, FASTER and more EXACT the marble rolls down that path. Reps create a "groove" in your nervous system, causing your techniques to come out "easier, faster and more exact" each time. And, just like riding a bike, you learn them so well it's hard to forget them.

FAQ #2: Why train with a grappling dummy at all? Why not just a live partner?

Although training partners are important for specific techniques and for "rolling", they aren't the most effective way to get high reps of many techniques. Here are 5 good reasons why:

1. You can only train when your partners are available. Grappling dummies are available 24/7. You can even get some decent reps in when you have just 5 minutes of spare time.

2. Partners can bring your training down to "slow motion". Partners want to talk about the techniques, "the fights on TV", etc. that's not the most effective use of your time and decreases the number of reps you get during the training session.

3. Partners have to do their reps. Right off the bat, this means you get only half the number of reps that you would if you were training on the grappling dummy.

4. The more reps your partner does on you, the more abuse to your joints. What do you think is the main reason people stop training? Injuries. It's a no brainer.

5. When was the last time your training partner let you do 50 triangle chokes on him, followed by 50 heel hooks, then 50 arm bars? Nuff said!

FAQ #3: Is training "in class" enough?

Have you ever taken music lessons? You had to have your instrument at home and practice between lessons, didn't you? And you couldn't practice just when you had someone over to practice with... otherwise it would have taken forever to get good. When you think of it like that, you really can't expect to become very good if you only practice in class, can you? It's only common sense. And a grappling dummy is your "instrument" that allows you to practice between lessons. It's like a boxer having a punching bag to train on in between sparring sessions.

© image courtesy of www.grapplingdummy.net

Reminder: Please be aware that I have no affiliation or interest in the businesses of Submission Master or Bob Dorris. Please revue various dummies that you feel might work best for you. This is only one perspective, but so happens it's a perspective I agree with and I've tested a few dummies over the years.

RECORDING

"If you can not measure it, you can not improve it." & "To measure is to know."
~ Lord Kelvin

The Lord was a little on the 'out there' side of things but to be honest with these two statements he was pretty much on the money. During the journey you will take over the next thirty days you will need to record a lot of the action. Not just for historical reasons so you can look back and see how well you did but also to keep you on track of the task at hand.

Let's go back to the map. We need to get from A to B. 'A' being where you are now in your BJJ Progression and 'B' being where you want to be - which should be better or much improved. Don't forget we need to make this improvement in a thirty-day period of time period or the subtitle for this book makes no sense!

The only way to see if progress is being made is via three things:
- Log or Journal
- Video
- Competition

We could put belt promotions in here but they vary so much from academy to academy that it cannot be held as a benchmark standard. I know the IBJJF would probably disagree but from what I've seen at tournaments not all blue belts (or any other belt for that matter) are created equal, so in the interests of a 30-day process let's keep promotions out as a measuring marker.

One thing I will say for promotions is that we grow into them. I heard the excellent black belt Shawn Williams speaking recently and he used this analogy: That most students sit (and fit) themselves into their rank, but when they are promoted they lift themselves to the new rank. Much like a plant being grown in a small pot, as the plant grows and expands it is transferred to a larger pot and this gives it the room to grow even more. If we view belt rankings as the pots then we grow into each pot through each phase of our development (promotion).

This came with the caveat that we also have to train; there is no avoiding training whichever way you slice it.

When it comes to recording your progress, you will notice more weak points than you could have held in your head. Also your Map will become an integral part of the Log. At the beginning of each week you will have a Preview and Review period. On Sunday (or pick a day that you won't forget) you can review your log and video content write some notes about what happened and the details you recorded and this then sets up the Preview. The Preview is a description of what you have planned coming up for the next week, your new goal (and orientation filter) for the coming period.

In this program you only have to do this P&R process four times. But you need to complete your journal after <u>every</u> session - no excuses. This will also become important when you get those, 'I don't think I can make it' days, the will to keep the progress and the cycle moving adds momentum. Don't break the chain!

If you don't complete your journal after each session then you will forget what happened in that session. Period. It's better to have a short pencil than a long memory. Also things change in your mind, maybe you notice a negative circuit pattern but you didn't get round to making a record of it then you need to go back and remember how you discovered the negative circuit. It will be hard to pin down exactly how the circuit played out as there are too many variable factors. When the technique and position are fresh in your mind it's easy to put it down on paper.

Be aware of this as you move forward in recording your progress.

I will cover the recording of Competition in the following section.

JOURNALS AND LOGS

Keeping a track of your progress is paramount if you are to improve in your jiu jitsu training. My professor recommends that if you improve by only 1% each day then the compounding effect will make you highly proficient in no time.

I have been keeping a training log for many years now and write down my efforts from the class just before I get into bed, this a little routine that now makes for interesting reading years later. I laugh at some of my goals and ambitions as a white and blue belt and laugh even more at some of the complex techniques I thought I might be able to manage - no kidding, there's a flying triangle in there.

Keeping a series of techniques in your head is a complex matter. This is human chess, for every attack there is a defense, for every sweep, takedown, pass, submission there is a counter and counter to that counter. It makes much more sense to keep taking notes than trying to remember what you did. Also, when you review (as you should periodically), some techniques you will identify as being easy to perform and fit your body-type. These techniques I put a star in the corner of the page and come back to drill some more. Then the techniques that present a challenge I put an X in the corner of the page, meaning I need to revisit that move and try and work out what detail I am missing that is making it so hard. The neutral techniques that I don't have a feeling of either way then I let them slide until I come back to them. These are my so-so techniques, I can do them but they don't fill me with joy.

This art form is a process and systems driven. One thing leads logically to another. It's the same position-transition-submission. Simple?

The logic though is lightning in a bottle. It needs to be grasped and placed into the correct place in the puzzle or the puzzle cannot be unlocked. Remember how a move was working really well and you were catching everyone or passing everyone, then a couple of weeks later it stopped working? What happened?? Probably, a detail you were applying has now been forgotten, wouldn't it be great if you could go back and retrieve the detail. You can. It's in your training log or journal.

Here's the cycle I discipline myself to implement:

Visualize - This is usually a demo from the coach or professor, or DVD or whatever. Then I see myself doing it, from my own perspective.
Practice - Try the technique out with a partner or grappling dummy. Go through the steps in meticulous detail.
Drill - If it works and 'no parts are missing' then I drill it up to 50-60 times.
Live Training / Test - Once it's working in my head I push myself into a sparring or specific training situation where I can test it. Usually the first couple of times out the gate it fails. Then it clicks and I test it as much as I can.

At the practice stage it enters the training log including the details that made it work so I can move to the drilling stage. If it doesn't work at the drilling stage, go back to the Practice stage and get the training journal out.

Sparring goes in the journal too. I don't spar without a goal in mind, so it's like a convoluted specific training. Convoluted in that, say my goal is back attacks then I have to go through the process of getting to the back before I can even begin to work my game.

Each element is important and should not be excluded. Once something works well in my game, I go back to cycle one - Visualize.

Here are some of the other benefits of using a training journal:

Memory - It's hard to remember all the techniques that you will be picking up in BJJ. This is a sport that is almost completely technique driven, yes, athleticism is a factor but you need the techniques regardless of your athletic prowess. At first the techniques can be a little overwhelming, and then you get the hang of it. As you move to more advanced techniques, again, it becomes a real battle of wits. Your journal is your memory backup. You drop your computer or spill coffee on it and the long-term data is a problem. With your journal or training log, you can drop it and then drop coffee all over and your jiu jitsu brain is safe.

Review - Goal setting is <u>not</u> one of my favorite things, I'm not a big 'goal guy'. I think this may be my aversion to the word and not necessarily what it means. You see, I feel it is imperative to have a point of focus for each session. In the early stages your professor and coach will provide this but as time wears on you'll need to motivate yourself to select techniques that fit your age, physical condition, body shape, weight, and many other factors. This is where you need to start getting creative.

Now if you set the focus of your training you need to check in and see how far along you've come. You can't just reminisce; it's got to be more solid than that. You need review sections in your training log that checks-in and keeps score. How's that half guard sweep coming along? You said you would have it mastered a month ago? Things like this accelerate your progress.

Trackback - Tracing your steps can be an important part of moving forward, especially if you are hitting a plateau. This re-visiting of your previous techniques and the times when your game felt really good can be a reminder that this could happen again in the future. Hitting a plateau can be very disheartening, a real slump pushed me to question whether to continue or not. Using my journal I decided to go back to basics and forget all the fancy techniques that were confusing me. This saved my BJJ career.

Here are some guidelines to keeping a good journal:

- Use symbols and marks that mean something to you. In the Zen Jiu Jitsu Training Log there is a box at the outside edge of the page. This is for you to add a star or check mark or cross to indicate this page is important in some way. That's the way I use the box, you might do something different. You might be creative enough to color the box a shade that reminds you how that training session went.

- Use shorthand. I use RNC in my notes that's an acronym for the Rear Naked Choke. It's a good idea to use TLA's (Three letter acronyms) in your journals, there's not a lot of space most of the time and when you don't feel like writing up the session due to exhaustion or other sweat-filled factors writing in shorthand really helps. Use TLA's or shorthand to describe your training partners and techniques, this makes for quicker entries.

- Make sure you get into a routine of adding the entries. Like I mentioned earlier I make sure I update my Training Log before I get into bed - on the night I trained. I don't try and remember the next day what I got up to. I try and write it down while it's fresh in my mind. You need to find a routine that works. One of the guys at my school gets his notebook out before he leaves the academy. It's covered in sweat that makes the ink blotchy. That's another tip: Use a pencil, I use a mechanical pencil and it works great, I do use the erasing department too.

- Keep a track on time. In the Zen Training Log we added a start and finish time. This records the overall time you committed to the class. But it also records when you had that class too, Wednesday evening from seven until nine. Great. And if you notice a pattern of stars in the box at the head of the page, then you might find that this is an optimal training time for you.

- Date the entries.

- I know this is repeating myself but it's important. Make sure each class has a goal or focus. Doesn't matter if it was set by the coach or professor or by you. Just make sure there is a focus and you're not just rolling around for the sake of it.

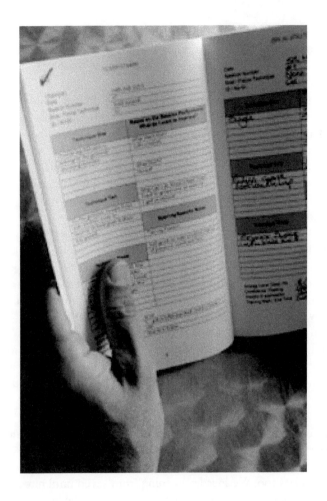

VIDEO RECORDING

Another great way of using technology to help you record your actions is the Video format. Next time you roll take your smart phone along or if you have the resources take your Flip video camera along. When you are going to spar and others are waiting or resting, ask one of your training partners to video your roll when he's having a rest between rounds.

This sounds a little silly when you first consider it but once you see yourself roll you'll be amazed. Have you ever played chess and one of the spectators seemed bemused by a move you made? Have you ever watched one of your teammates at a tournament and saw him do something that seemed totally random, or out of character? Or missed a sub that was staring him in the face? Or let himself get subbed when the escape was right there!?

Of course we have, because we have a wider perspective from the outside.

One of the reasons you get caught in an obvious sub or miss an opportunity is that you are in the thick of the action. It's much easier to assess things from a third party objective perspective.

This is how this video system works, only you are your own coach and own critic. The last words of the Buddha went something like this 'shine a light onto yourself'. What he meant was be your own advocate, be your own coach, analyze and watch your own actions ... wake up! Don't just accept the advice of others ... look deeper. It's okay for a coach to tell you where you went wrong when you get caught or miss a position, but when you see it ... a picture is literally worth a thousand words.

This was a real eye opener for me the first time I did it. Actually I went around the houses a little and started off by getting one of my training buddies to take some stills with my phone. The technology was not as good then even with the iPhone, you could only just about take photos, but it did give me a little more insight into my game. Then when video became available I started to film some of my rolling sessions (well not really me filming but a colleague or one of the moms who had come to pick up a kid, basically anyone not rolling) this was a big help.

It's my recommendation that you start to video some of your drilling sessions first. This will help you with some details and positions plus it's much more non-threatening. Take this into consideration. If you hand your phone to someone on the sideline and say can you video this, your opponent will feel slightly threatened plus you will probably want to be the star of the video. You need to explain its part of a BJJ improvement program you are trying out, but be aware the ego is a strong and powerful beast.

Now, if you just start by filming your drilling (non-threatening) and then just upgrade to rolling no one will hardly notice. This is just a tip from the top. If you go to a new school and tell some sideliner 'Hey, video me rolling with this kid.' Then 'this kid' will more than likely try to smash you big time. Be aware that it's polite to ask someone to be filmed or recorded in any way.

Also don't think this a green light to beat up on the White Belts so you have a video collection of 'Beatdowns', this is a purely a training aid ... and a very good one if not abused.

In fact, the video format works better when you roll with people much better than you. If you keep getting caught and broke apart by one of your teammates catch it next time on your Flip or iPhone and then dismantle your game to see where you went wrong. Also see how your teammate plays, what are his strengths and weaknesses. I bet the next time you roll, you'll show some technical abilities that surprise him. Next thing you know all your training partners are videoing their progress ... and you are the trendsetter.

ATTENTION TO SELF

Zen students study for many years before they are allowed to teach others. It's a very long road to become a Zen master. A monk who had recently become a teacher was traveling and stumbled across a monastery in the countryside. As it turned out it was the monastery of a master he had studied under many years before. He went in and set up tea with his old master, hoping to impress him with how far he come in his studies, and he now was also a Zen master.

It was the rainy season, so as he traveled he wore rain shoes and carried an umbrella. He left them in the hallway and went though to see his old master. They exchanged greetings, the master asked "In the hallway, did you leave your umbrella on the left or on the right of your rain shoes?"

The new teacher was unaware of how he had left his umbrella, and then realized he had much further to travel in his journey of self realization.

How is it that so many people get countered in Jiu Jitsu? In fact not just Jiu Jitsu but just about every martial art has a plethora of counter attacks, we can include chess in this maxim too. A simple guard pass counter seems to be one of the most effective counters there is. In many a match I don't do anything, I know my counter, set up the guard I know will suck the opponent in and bam! I'm working my game. One of the main reasons this happens is due to the overload of attention units.

Assume that your mind can only hold a specific number of attention units before your mind starts to wander and you lose concentration altogether. These are actual units in number and the number is individual to each person.

When you move to pass guard your attention is on the guard pass. And usually the majority of your attention units are absorbed by grips, pressure and balance assigned to that pass. This usually means that you are not 'Observing' your opponent with all that much attention. When your pass gets blocked or is foiled, you adapt quickly to the situation and try to recover back to your starting position (scramble).

How many times have you had to post from a sweep? If your opponent had only gripped that arm or leg you would have flipped through the air with ease. This is lack of Observation due to the absorption of attention units. Your attention is still on the guard pass even after it failed.

When you move to pass don't place ALL your attention units on the pass from your side, get a feel for their (your opponents) position too, especially the hips. In fact you should place as little attention as possible on the passing technique and keep all other attention units free, this will prevent any surprise attacks.

This creates the atmosphere of good split focus. You direct your attention at your partner looking for good attacking possibilities and setting up your guard game while Observing for counter responses. This is hard to do, but will put you light years ahead your competition. (Review the section on Observation).

Don't forget when you are sparring you have to monitor yourself as much as you have to monitor your opponent. Don't fall asleep. How many times have you asked a training partner who has a great sweep, "That was a cool sweep, how did you position for that?" and they reply "Not sure." I've had that happen so many times it's hard to believe. Also you can tell when an opponent is grunting and using all the strength they have. Their attention units have collapsed and they have no other options. This style of sparring is based in fear. Their ego is based on the 'W'!

This also applies to why you get swept or triangled from the same technique over and over again. If you realized and were self aware enough to recognize the opening you created you just wouldn't do it again.

Being self-aware is the state of knowing what you are doing at all times without having a rigid control of yourself. Awareness not rigidity.

Rigidity is the basis for the fear mode. You never make a mistake because you never make anything. If you finish a sparring session without being tapped or improving your position on at least one of your training partners you might as well as not bothered sparring. There is no improvement in the rigid mind set. Get tapped, improve a position, or its just a workout. Rolling is the time to be risky, just be mindful that you are being risky.

When you create a certain amount of awareness, you can see the mistakes you make, you know why those mistakes happened and then you can find out how to correct them. Go back to your maps, video journals and logs. Watch yourself and watch your opponent, you'll get the hang of this on no time.

Please, please, please, do not focus on strength, or focus on how much strength you use in each technique. Muscle is the opposite of mindfulness. How many Buddhist monks arm wrestle? Stay cool, and if you screw up, Tap, say to yourself 'Relax', touch knuckles and go again.

ROLLING

This is the fun part right! After all what's the use of drilling, mastering technique if you never get a chance to sample the goods on anyone? This is true but as with all parts of this text I have a few suggestions.

Next time you roll decide your game plan before you actually play. Think about your weekly preview, what have you been working on? What's the Go-To move that you would like to improve and see if it works? This is a better system than what I see at most academies. A lot of BJJ students seem to roll aimlessly! Next time you are going to roll ask these two questions of your partner, "Do you have any injuries, anything I need to watch?" and "What are you working on? You want to work toward a position?"

I always ask these before every roll, the first question is respectful, this is my training partner, if he has sore ribs from a prior roll then I don't go in for side smash passes. If his fingers are swollen then I'm easy on grip breaks. The second question is more telling. Virtually 90% of all the team members you roll with will answer "Nah, nothing much, let's just roll."

Now they are either guarding their game plan, they might not want you to know they have a killer Berimbolo move ready to strike, but the chances are that your partner is just 'rolling' around. This is ineffective training. The whole ethos of BJJ was based on minimum effort equals maximum result, using leverage to create a favorable position or as described in most business situations this is described as: Efficiency.

Rolling around on the ground with sweaty guys is not a statement I could find in any books on efficiency. Believe me, I've looked. A valid game plan before you begin is efficient.

There is nothing to say your game plan will prove to be efficient. Especially if it's your first outing for a particular technique, it's bound to be fraught with missed details, poor leverage, timid execution, but as you drill and become more confident then this situation will change. Time on the mats is a huge part of this equation to become one thousand percent improved in thirty days and that's the goal. The end result.

Make sure that when you roll you keep it technical at all times. If you hit the mat for the sparring session and feel tension in your body then it is not a good sign that you will be loose enough to get technical. If your face feels tense and you can't crack a smile with your training partner, no matter what, then you need to slow down. You'll never get through thirty days of rolling if every training session is a World Championship, life or death, bout.

Being technical helps you relax. It's much easier to roll when you have an idea of what you are doing or plan to do. If you are a white belt you may still be in the 'I don't know what I don't know' phase, and this is good, enjoy it. You will need to tap ten thousand times before you reach your black belt ... so start now, get a few taps under your belt. Some students don't want to tap regardless of the position they are in. They hold out, they have horrendous injuries, and then they stop training. This is a totally inefficient system in my book (and this is my book).

In Jiu Jitsu we have a perfect system for stopping the action when your partner pulls of a great technique – you tap. You should celebrate your mat buddy having the smarts to pull off this move ... shake hands, touch knuckles and go again ... get tapped again. It's all good.

Do I get tapped with my game plan, my excessive drilling, my technical moves like a chess master? All the time ... and I like it.

Why? Consider the alternative. You take up a more concussive martial art, let's say Muay Thai. There is no tap. You'll take some lumps and dish some out but if your opponent is more advanced than you then be prepared to take a considerable thumping. Jiu Jitsu has a more elegant stop process. It's well determined and defined, two taps, verbal inclusive as well as foot taps stop the process and we can begin again.

Try going all out Muay Thai seven nights a week without getting some serious injuries and maybe a little brain damage. Most striking art schools would not permit full contact between teammates for this very reason, so see yourself in a very fortunate position, leave your ego at the door and tap when it necessitates it.

THINKING PROCESSES WHILE SPARRING

Let's go back to the brain-as-computer analogy. We take in bits and pieces of data and file them in their appropriate places in our brains. The problem with most BJJ students is that they file a lot of the information under 'miscellaneous', or it gets lost.

Okay, so let's see if we can make better use of the computer filing system.

1. Observe your Opponent. Most fighters have styles that they like, roll with someone long enough and you'll get a handle on his or her circuits and that will leave you the option to counter. Most of your sparring partners will have 'a game' and it will become obvious. Unfortunately most practitioners don't even consider this, even if they were told what was going to happen beforehand.

2. What does your opponent do when you attack? Does he pull guard, put up a knee shield, roll out, hip out, etc? What does he do the most often? Most fighters have five or less defensive patterns that they are comfortable with. Jiu Jitsu is infinite so everyone needs a comfort zone, it's not like Boxing or Karate where there a set number of options (jab, cross, kick, block) this is a whirling series of connected events, so humans need patterns until the number perplexes them, this is usually four or five and then maybe another eight they can scrape by with but don't have command over.

3. Do this exercise. Pick four or five of your classmates and watch them spar; see if you can see which guard they prefer. See if you can see whether they prefer top or bottom or to sweep, watch in real detail. Which foot did they use for the sweep? Which hand was the influential grip? Did they have good balance? Did they

shake (muscle tremor style) as if they were trying to balance or out-muscling their opponent? Try and notice everything. Style habits are easy to spot.

4. If they go straight on the attack, which side did they attack with first? What pass were they aiming at? Knee cutter, standing pass, etc. How close/near were they for the attack?

This is a lot to remember, but once you get into the habit it gets really (really) easy. Use the protocol outlined in 'Objective Analysis', which should make this process easier.

This is one of the hardest things for a fighter to do. Look at a match with a detached introspection - no emotional additives. Keep an eye what you get scored on plus the factors involved and what you score with. This is the process that leads to excellence.

TECHNIQUE

Technical ability in Jiu Jitsu, to me at least, is the pinnacle. I've seen small technical Jiu Jitsu practitioners with little or no athletic ability absolutely murder younger, larger opponents who depend on strength too much.

'Technique conquers all' to quote the BJJ phenom Caio Terra. This is a guy winning Absolutes at one hundred and thirty pounds. Which, regardless of whether you like Caio or not, is nothing short of impressive.

Having a technical base is important to your game, and to your future in Jiu Jitsu. If you have a couple of Go-To moves, have a good gas tank and hold a little muscle this is a great start to making positive waves in your academy. But if that is where it stays, the picture will surely change with the passing of time. As your team bypass your technical ability and have an answer to your Go-To moves you'll find that you can spar all night due to your athleticism but you'll also get subbed a ton. That blue belt doesn't hang too well now and if you don't get your brain in the game then you'll more than likely wash out of the BJJ system before purple hits your waistline.

If you are athletic don't let that be you. If you are not athletic (like me) then you need to be technical, there is no other way!

Results will take care of themselves if the technique (Process) is put in correctly. The famous motivational speaker Jim Rohn said *"Success is nothing more than a few simple disciplines, practiced every day; while failure is simply a few errors in judgment, repeated every day."*

I am convinced after the varying amounts of research I've had to wade through to get this manual in shape that focusing on <u>process</u>

<u>(technique) is the key</u>. The alternative is focusing on the result, the win. But the problem is that the win, the end result is often times out of our control and this is never a good thing whereas processes are always within our grasp. Focus on processes (technique) and the result will come.

Masters and PGA Golf Champion Jackie Burke, Jr., used two equations to represent the relationship between process [P] and results [R]. He said that P over R = $, and that R over P = Zero. A simple formula, which basically meant that if you put results (submissions, say, at all cost) over process (the drilling of techniques) then you'll end up nowhere. If you reverse the formula you'll hit gold.

This process is one that I think fits nicely into the ethos behind Zen Jiu Jitsu, it's the principle behind the attitude and protocol I'm suggesting here.

OBJECTIVE ANALYSIS

Try this. An objective analysis of a BJJ Match. Go to YouTube (there are thousands) pick one of your favorites and then view the match from one side. Pick your player, like a video game; you are him for this match. Write down your thoughts as the match unfolds.

Next, look at the match as a detached observer. Think strategy and what could have been done to improve. You can have no subjective input at all; you have to leave any support or ego for your player at the door. You are like his coach, your opinions have nothing to do with the outcome of the match. Write down every technique, sweep and submission attempt or sub that happened - keep it all mechanical.

Got it? Good.

Now use the same exercise but with one of the videos you shot of yourself in the Recording section of the manual.

No emotion can come into it. It has to be purely mechanics. Watch the video footage as if it is not you but your video game buddy. See how emotional you and your opponent are on the mat but do not react in your run down of the mechanics (what happened), again write down every technique, sweep, transition, position and result.

Got it? Good.

First order of business, "Where are you?" (It's the old Observation routine again.)

As I mentioned in the first chapter, the most important factor you have to be aware of in any sparring situation is where you are.

Are you in half guard? Are you on top, bottom, in side control? Where are your grips?

Second in line is, "What's going on?"

Are you winning or losing? What's going well and not so well? You have to be accurate when you are recording this, you can easily spot how you didn't post your hand, your balance was off, your hips were too high, you didn't have grips etc.,

Let's get specific.

What happens to you in each position? Are you moving into different positions or favoring one position? Which guard did you start with? What is the pattern of the match from starting guard to submission or time-out?

Once you have these two in order, the next question is "How?" How did you get into this position? How did your opponent score or fall into your counter? How did he set you up, does he stand to pass, is his right or left leg forward. Remember: be meticulous. How are you taking advantage of his guard position? Which side do you present forward, do you pull guard or do you go for the top? Are you comfortable?

We've covered, where, what and how. Let's look at the "When" of the session. What is the timing involved? Slow, Fast, Easy, Hard?

From the beginning of the crossing exchange (Critical Distance Line), where grips are established 1) Does he break your grip and move forward, or 2) Do you initiate the first attack? In the middle of the action, 3) Do you sweep to move on top, 4) Are you reversed to the bottom position? Did you hesitate? Are there periods of a lull because you are not sure how to respond to his position? Is the hesitation or pause long or short? Is this due to resting, are you tired? How is your balance throughout?

Look for general overarching factors, what position does everyone get you in? And then work on the specifics. What move did you fall for? What position were you in when you knew the counter but didn't use it, or just plain forgot the technique? What is proving the most successful pattern in your sparring?

When you put all this together, the Where, What, How and When you will begin to see patterns emerge, the good and bad.

Example: Your opponent attempts to pass your butterfly guard and you pull to half guard (Where) he pushes his weight on top of you and takes head control, you still feel pretty comfortable and in control (What). You take advantage of the weight and slide your right side hip underneath to recover full guard (How). He presses his weight forward again resisting the sweep but allows your knee to slide through and you complete the recovery by switching your hips back and forth to full guard (When).

It's easy to do with a little practice and a keen eye - to recap:

1.   Watch a good match on YouTube, or record some footage in the Academy.
2.   Record your own match
3.   Roll slow and Analyze the positions generally
4.   Review the recording and Analyze the positions specifically
5.   Rotate 2 and 3 speeding up the roll as you go
6.   Do not explore new positions you until you feel comfortable in the ones you just analyzed (see Drilling)

When students roll they get caught up in a lot of emotion and reaction to their surroundings for most of the time. Getting caught by a stupid sweep you never normally get caught with and you might hear yourself say, "Just not concentrating tonight..." or "A little tired from the previous roll...took my eye off the ball."

The real skill here is being able to analyze and roll in the full heat of the battle with detached calmness. This is when you see World Champions who are several moves ahead of their competitors. If you follow the above processes of analysis before and after sparring then this will speed up this process no end. You need the ability to spot circuit patterns in yourself and your opponent and then to adjust those patterns to the match you are in. It's simple: You analyze and adapt. Adapt or Die!

What if you opponent doesn't play ball and won't fit into the pattern of your favorite position? How many times have you seen the killer guard player falter because he gets guard pulled on <u>him</u>!?

You have to customize your approach to his greatest number of weaknesses. Nullify his defense and exploit his weakness. It's simple warfare.

How do you do this? Just ask: Where, What, How and When.

Start looking at what you are doing. Start looking at what your training partner is doing. Use the strongest muscle in your body - your brain - to become fully engaged in this process. When you have a good roll with no objective and you just roll around getting a good sweat then that's all this session could ever be ... a good workout. You cannot gain any understanding.

When you start to apply logic and have a goal before each session you will jump to a level you did not expect (or your teammates expect) in short order.

Do not roll on instinct. Not in the early stages - and that's all the way up to Brown Belt.

Do not pull a particular guard, do not sweep or counter or recover guard unless *you decide* to do any of those things. The trick to winning an exchange is to get your opponent to play *your* game, not the other way around. If you control *your* own actions then ostensibly you control the match.

CHAPTER THREE: DEVELOPMENT

Now you have all the components to jump your game to the next level and improve 1000%, we need to consider the long term. Staying in the BJJ game is easier said than done, maybe one of the reasons to drop out is due to injury or lack of conditioning or motivation. These are the most common elements that make people wash out of the system.

Here are some pointers to help you keep moving to the next level and beyond.

365 DAY CHALLENGE

This was how this 30 day system developed. I saw an article in the local newspaper that reported a girl had been surfing for 365 straight days in a year. That's 365 straight, not massaging the figures so it was 365 surf sessions in a year ... every day ... no crying, no bailouts. Straight.

Could this be possible within Jiu Jitsu? This is where my mind went as soon as I read the article. Would it possible to roll every day for a whole year, that would take some real commitment and I thought I might be the man to test it!

Was I successful? Yes and No.

For some reason, I felt it would be useful to start this exercise on my Birthday. I had to manage several other factors too, like my academy was not open seven days a week and working out at other academies was not allowed. That's where Burt (my submission dummy) came in. Fit and well, I could embark on this journey and see where the wind took me.

The program was great and I was flying along for the first month. Regardless of other commitments I made sure that I had a Jiu Jitsu session every day. Then the second month came along, I had decided to work harder on this protocol and seriously included drilling in my program as well as visiting other schools regardless of my own association rules. By the third month there were whispers around my own academy that I had been traveling North for private lessons with another Professor ... no one improves so much in such a short time, right?

My skills in psychology improved and I got my roadmap in real shape. From being a very mediocre Blue Belt I accelerated into my Purple Belt without even looking back. I honed the technique even further, still rolling or drilling every day.

My rules to qualify for a BJJ session every day: it had to be for a minimum of one hour. I followed the thirteen year old girl from the newspaper ... no excuses ... every day.

Then I made a couple of small errors, not in my method but in new techniques I tested. I had not drilled them enough and my confidence was at an all time high, I picked up a small injury, then another. It was my hand but serious enough to affect my grip. This didn't faze me I adapted and carried on, then a rib injury due to a white belt losing his balance and dropping his weight when we were practicing. He didn't even realize it wasn't his fault. His 250 pound knee fell on me while I wasn't even looking never mind concentrating.

Undeterred I rallied on, reducing my sparring time and concentrating on more of the psychology. I managed my training partners to lighter guys, felt like I could roll when Bam!! My back called it quits. The program was over ... for a short while at least.

This was a very difficult time. Long periods of inactivity don't work very well with my stress levels. My day job is moderately active and involves long periods of driving, but getting in and out of the driving seat proved almost impossible.

I had been using my journal effectively so I went back and reviewed the previous six months. What a ride, and that's when I decided to document this work. As a lifetime Buddhist I thought it would be cool for someone to consider the mind and psychology of Jiu Jitsu and that's when Zen Jiu Jitsu was born.

All the lessons I learned in the improving of my game I broke down, used my background in the sciences to cover the learning steps and put them together in a structured fashion. This manual was a long time in the making and that back injury was a long time ago but the lessons are as vivid today as they were then.

So what did I learn from a marathon Jiu Jitsu session? It is possible to train forever.

If someone had written this text and I had read it beforehand I could have lasted the year. It is doable, and I want someone to do it and prove it can be done. I'm not that man anymore, not because I couldn't do it, now I have the tools but my motivation has changed and although BJJ is a massive part of my life, to complete the 365 day challenge you have to recognize beforehand that your life will be out of balance for quite some time.

For younger people, balance isn't such a big deal. But if you have a family, a mortgage, a day job, this kind of undertaking (if taken seriously) can be damaging. And nothing is worth that.

That's why the 30 day program is ideal. You will get maximum benefit from a limited effort. In other words it is a maximally efficient program.

If you are young, don't need the balance, and want to kill the competition then try it for a year. Your progress will be astonishing. But please ensure you read the whole manual first, then maybe read it again before you make the commitment public. There are pitfalls as well as the potential for huge gains in your game.

It's 30 days minimum then break. If you complete the 30 days and want to go on then you will need to understand, digest and absorb the information that follows.

INJURY MANAGEMENT

You need to be respectful of your body at all times. Without this amazing device that we take for granted most of the time, you have no game, you have no BJJ, you are just an inactive lump of fat and muscle tissue taking in daytime TV.

WARNING!
<u>Do Not</u> knowingly damage this device (no not your Kindle or iPad, your body). That means be careful what you put in it from food to drugs. Your game and your life depend on it - literally.

This Jiu Jitsu thing is a long-term proposition. We only have to look at the founders Helio and Carlos to know this can be practiced into a ripe old age. Not only that, but as we practice when we're older we can still be effective and vibrant as older people. This is a wonderful sport for staying young.

With the above statement in mind, and a protocol in your hand that encourages a contact sport on a daily basis for a whole month, you need to manage any injuries that may flare or are pre-existing.

ICE is your friend.
Icing an injured body part is an important part of treatment. Icing injuries can be effective for sprains, strains, overuse injuries and bruises. Learn how to properly ice your injury.

Using ice to recover from an injury is nothing new. You just need to learn how to use the ice properly.

Get the ice on as soon as the injury presents itself. Most schools have ice packs waiting for any flare-ups or joint pops. Don't be macho and don't wait. The benefits of icing being effective reduce significantly over a 48-hour period.

Ice Massage. Move the ice around, do not allow it to sit in one place.

Elevate. If the body part can be raised, make sure it's higher than the heart during the ice massage. This should further reduce any swelling. If it's a lower back injury, to alleviate pressure when you lie down make sure you have a pillow beneath your knees and you feet up at 90 degrees (if possible). Like being sat on a chair but with your back on the ground.

Timing. 15 minutes is the ideal time to massage. No longer. The results are diminishing from there and can even cause more damage if this is not respected. Frostbite can also be an issue.

Rest. Also you need to have a good rest period between massages. Once you have massaged the area leave it 45 minutes to an hour before the next ice massage.

Repeat. Keep going through this process but do not ice massage if the area still feels cold. The area must have returned to normal body temperature before the next icing is initiated.

Helpful Ideas:

1. Use a plastic bag with crushed ice for the massage or to rest ice on a knee for example. The crushed ice will mold around body parts. You can also use a bag of frozen peas or corn, this also works.
2. Buy some paper cups filled with water and a peel off lid then freeze them. These are ideal ice massage devices. Peel the top off and massage the muscle area with circular motions, this will induce a nice even cool area in no time.
3. Don't allow the ice to just sit on the skin as this can induce frostbite. If it's more ligament based like a knee or finger/thumb injury (which are common) then apply the ice massage and then rest it for a few seconds then remove then massage then rest and repeat but DO NOT leave any form of ice just resting on the skin, always put a towel or cloth between ice and skin.
4. The reason why ice is so effective especially for soft tissue injuries is that it reduces swelling and inflammation by reducing blood flow to the injured area. It can also reduce pain a little if the injury is quite serious.

WHEN TO GET HELP?

If your injury is not showing any signs of improvement or even feeling worse within a few days then please go to see a physician. If the pain in the injury is acute and regardless of icing the pain does not subside then go to see your physician right away.

Tapping 10,000 Times

One of the aims of this program is to get you tapped 10,000 times. If you can achieve this then I promise you (absolutely guarantee it) that you will be an A1 Jiu Jitsu player – and probably a Black Belt as that would take quite some time. The trick is staying in the game long enough to get tapped 10K times. This needs management and watching how you train and the injuries you sustain from small easy fixes to potential surgery.

At all costs avoid surgery. I don't know one player who came back from surgery better than they were previously. My physician explained this to me and it's pretty simple: The body is a sealed container, it's like the black box computer on board a BMW or Porsche, it's not meant for the owner or even some Joe Blow mechanic to come along and open it up.

Once opened the seal can never be truly put back. There is so much bacteria and energy in the world, even in an operating theatre that a hundred years from now civilization will look back and consider the current mode of surgery as barbaric. Avoid this at all costs. Rest, recover. If it looks like you need major surgery then consider that Jiu Jitsu will more than likely become a hobby for you in the future. Keep it simple and enjoy rolling ... and please don't incur another injury that would need surgical help.

PATIENCE, HISTORY, PHILOSOPHY

In tennis this is a standard term. One that if you decide to go for the 365 day route will need to be aware of:

This technique involves dividing training periods of up to a year (the macrocycle) into smaller periods (mesocycles), which are then divided further into microcycles.

Each period or cycle might be a mini training program in and of itself lasting 6 weeks or more.
This approach is intended to avoid overtraining and result in a peak in performance at tournament time.

Each has its own goal and one cycle follows sequentially on from the other. Like in many other sports, tennis demands many different types of strength ... in particular muscular endurance/resistance and explosive execution of power. A foundation is needed to achieve loftier goals.

To read more on periodization try:
http://www.tenniscruz.com/periodization-in-tennis/#ixzz22tMtY41D

In Jiu Jitsu this is even harder as injuries play such a high factor. You need to build breaks, rest periods into your schedule ahead of time. You also need to break training down into smaller components of higher intensity mixed in with lower intensity. You cannot roll hard for thirty days, it will kill you if you don't get injured and fall by the wayside before the thirty days are up.

Get your thirty-day schedule and then look at the first week. You should be able to see when you can train and you can probably work out the advanced classes, competition classes and fundamentals (beginners classes). So let's say that your schedule looks like this:

Mon - Advanced
Tues - Fundamental
Wed - Advanced
Thurs - School Closed
Fri - Lunchtime No Gi
Sat - Competition Class
Sun - No-Gi Comp Class

This is a heavy week. I would say that there is only Tuesday and Thursday that look low intensity. The others could work out hard or easy depending who shows up to roll. Also on Thursday you will be drilling, so even though I have considered that low-intensity, it's still a tough workout.

Sticking to this plan for thirty days will leave you exhausted and sore at the end of the period. In fact even with some periodization locked in you will still be pretty sore at the end of the process regardless. I always tell students that regardless of the process build in rest at the end of the thirty-day protocol. If you are going beyond that, days thirty-one to thirty five, should be drilling and fundamentals only. No heavy rolling activity in this time, this should allow your body to recover a little.

It might be worth looking at the schedule above and building in more drilling. I would move Sunday to another drilling session, this will prime the pump and allow review time for a heavy roll on Monday, then you have low-Intensity (LI) class on Tuesday with the Fundamentals (lots of white belt action). Some students who are higher grades think that dropping to a fundamentals class is a waste of time, but I (and my own Professor) believe the opposite. It can be helpful and really sharpen your game to review and revisit all the fundamental techniques that you probably still use in your more advanced BJJ sessions.

Remember the section on Drilling (how could you forget), constantly repeating techniques is the KEY to improving your Jiu Jitsu. This is a double scoop in the instance of a regular practitioner with lower ranking belts, the rolling is more technical for you, it has to be and the competition not as stiff as there are plenty of lower belts trying to work out their own game. If you keep super technical then these lower belts should have a lot of trouble with your position. It's a real eye opener when you get a little sloppy or use strength and a real strong guy gives you a hard time. Time for a re-think.*

This is considered a LI session for the sake of this part of the manual.

When you move to an advanced class, work your game and work it full on. Even if you roll with a good buddy who you don't want to smash, that's fine, this is the gentle art - keep it technical. This is the watchword for the whole system - technique. If you sweep and submit someone, use his or her balance as a weapon and keep the submission clean (as in not jaw breaking, or applying a face bar as opposed to a RNC) then you and he/she both improve ... and enjoy the process. If he gets the better of you - excellent! This is now an escape you need to work as part of your map.

When I was initially developing the system I got caught in a foot lock, twice, by the same person during a round. Twice?

This made me think and then add it to my map. I built it into my drilling session, found the YouTube video that had the solution and spent one hour on nothing but this escape. I happened across my buddy at another sparring session a couple of weeks later, he went for the foot lock again and boom I was free. He tried to counter; I was ready and came on top. Not only did he give me props and laugh about it but also it totally moved him out of his rhythm. If we had been in a competition situation, he had screwed himself by falling asleep with the foot lock so confident was he that he could pull it off.

We discussed the technique afterwards and he had been drilling the technique many times, but hadn't drilled the counter to my escape. He added it to his map for the next time.

Periodization, using LI and HI techniques are the best way to get the most out of your sparring and drilling sessions. Use the time wisely.

*: This happened to me last night. I got sloppy and a bodybuilder type just bench-pressed me out of position. I thought the process through. Arrogance and hubris paid me a visit - a nice little reminder.

REST AND RECOVERY

Within the periodization section I mentioned that if you plan to extend your program beyond thirty days then when you get to day thirty, days thirty-one to thirty-five should only be drilling and fundamentals classes, essentially low intensity (LI) classes. This is important.

If you are <u>not</u> extending the program have two days off completely, have dinner with a loved one, savor the achievement of the last thirty days, read a good book, have fun, go to the gym but don't go to the academy. We only have a short break to re-stoke the fire before we get back to our BJJ addiction.

Then the next three days should be a reintroduction to training: drilling and fundamentals so go back to your more intense workouts on day six. You can transition back into your regular training set whatever it is, three or four days per week or one day on / one day off. However you train that works for you.

Or you can go back to another thirty-day challenge.

The R & R period though prevents two things:
1. Injuries
2. Burnout

We talked about Injuries in the section on Injury Management; the next phase goes into more depth on what Burnout is.

THE OPPOSITE OF BURNOUT

The opposite of burnout is peak performance. It's true that a lot of athletes aim to hit peak performance around a particular event or competition but what if there is no deadline ... No Olympics, No Pans, No World Champs, No Nationals? Maybe you just want to be a strong BJJ player, you enjoy the camaraderie and workout. But you still want to be good at the game ... and that means playing it smart.

This is the definition of burnout according to Dr Robert Neff from his excellent book 'Roadmap to the Zone'

ATHLETIC BURNOUT !

Physical Signs: Feelings of exhaustion, a lingering cold, frequent gastrointestinal problems (stomach aches), frequent headaches, sleeplessness, shortness of breath and/or strange weight loss.

Behavioral Signs: Quick temper, instantaneous frustration, feeling overburdened (first thought of the day is "Oh, no!"), inability to hold feelings in, yelling and screaming, feelings of helplessness, giving up easily, loss of caring for loved ones, greater risk taking behavior and consistently decreased performances.

Sport Related Signs: Reduced feel for the skill or movement, never happy with performance, start to expect bad performances, slower reactions, increased unforced errors over many competitions, difficulty focusing (poor concentration/eye control), treat coach and team mates like strangers and with general impatience.

Ideal Candidate for Burnout: A dedicated, overachiever with an external focus of control (does things for other people or for extrinsic rewards) or a person with extreme role conflict or role ambiguity (doesn't understand herself or how she fits into a variety of situations) [Fender (1989), Athlete burnout, The Sport Psychologist, 3 (1), pp. 63-71].

Burnout Avoidance

1) Become more aware of the symptoms and underlying causes of each
2) Cross training (use other related sports to help accomplish your fitness goals)
3) Day(s) off (proper "periodization training" should include days off)
4) Change of scenery (different practice location, inside vs. outside, road trips)
5) Support from others (friends, family, coach)
6) Work directly with a sport psychologist
7) Tournament scheduling (allow time to rest and recover)
8) Practice scheduling (quality not just quantity)
9) Proper goal setting (focus only on things you can control)

As you can see Athletic Burnout can happen to anyone. You don't have to be a high level player of any sport; you could be just busting your hump to be the best you can be. But you need balance, and you need to sometimes be aware that you are out of balance. Look out for these signs and you should be in a position to look after yourself and remedy it.

HUMAN CHESS

"The great world chess champion Emmanuel Lasker once said that it is not so much playing the objectively best move that is important as playing the move that is most undesirable for a particular opponent." David Levy, International Chess Grand Champion, Omni, April 1979.

Thinking about the Jiu Jitsu sparring process I cannot imagine a better analogy than human chess. There are many variables for the human element, like strength and cardio. These are elements that most chess grand masters don't need to worry about, but as BJJ practitioners we do. Then there are the technical aspects. Just like the quote above from David Levy the process of winning a match in chess and winning a match in Jiu Jitsu is the same.

Attack, defend, counter, counter to the counter, and so on.

Patterns begin to form which we have discussed ad-nausea in earlier sections. As the patterns begin to form we have a plan (a pattern, a circuit) to combat them. In chess they have really cool names, names for openings, names for middle game patterns and then end-game patterns. Things like the nimzo-indian defense and other cool names that I wished BJJ patterns had.

If you take a match that you have analyzed and it demonstrates the pattern:
Pull half-guard, push for old school, opponent pushes back with weight, under-sweep, move to side-control.

We could call this the 'half-old-school-defense' or some other name that doesn't just describe a technique but a definitive pattern. This might sound a little hokey, it did to me, but as we worked on various patterns and linked them together as more than just techniques or positions, the patterns became easier to remember.

This is what happens in chess schools. At first the students have to learn how all the pieces move (the techniques, or fundamentals in the cognitive phase) and then they learn how to open a match properly, middle game strategies (usually scrambles at this phase) and then the end-game (in BJJ these are positions, transitions and submissions) and then they link them all together depending on how the game is flowing they choose different strategies. In Jiu Jitsu we call this ... er ... we don't have a name for it, so random rolling becomes the norm.

In boxing the coaches are constantly encouraging their fighters to put combinations together. They want their boxers to think in terms of 3,4,5 and not just the good ol' 1,2, jab cross combo. In Jiu Jitsu a lot of the time we are left to our own devices but maybe we should think beyond the guard-break, pass to side control, and then what ... stall for a little. Then again, if that is super successful maybe you should go with it.

It worked for Roger Gracie for years: sweep to half guard to mount to cross-choke – game over. Worked like a charm year in year out, yet I've never seen anyone else repeat the process. That's why it's important to take the phenoms and freaks (in the nice sense of the word) out of the bell curve. If you're a genius, just roll with it, if you're like me - a normal human being - then think beyond the basics. Once you have the core fundamentals under control then come up with a chain of events that will take you all the way to the submission.

WHAT WE CAN LEARN FROM FIGHT CLUB?

Honestly. Not much. But if we look at Jiu Jitsu as a more expressive art form then we can combine some philosophy and expression into the fighting art. This is where Fight Club comes in. Tyler Durden really wanted the space monkeys to express themselves and free themselves by using fighting as a natural component of expression. I know that's a little deep but the film was quite explicit in some of its ideas and some of the ideas are valid and pertain to your training. Maybe not directly, but as you become more experienced some of them may resonate with you. Here are some of Tyler's gems. I know this because Tyler knows this:

- First rule of fight club, don't talk about fight club.*
- No fear. No distractions. The ability to let that, which does not matter, truly slide.
- I say never be complete, I say stop being perfect, I say let's evolve, let the chips fall where they may.
- It's only after we have lost everything that we're free to do anything.
- You're not your job. You are not how much money you have in the bank. You are not the car you drive. You are not the contents of your wallet. You are not your fucking khakis.
- People do it every day, they talk to themselves ... they see themselves as they'd like to be, they don't have the courage you have to just run with it.
- Sticking feathers up your butt does not make you a chicken.

And most importantly...

- This is your life, and it's ending one minute at a time.

*: This has no relationship to Jiu Jitsu at all but I think it's pretty cool.

THE ANTI-YOU

Keith Owen gives a great talk about the Anti-You on YouTube, the link is in the reference section. This was the first time I was exposed to this idea but thought it was an important addition to this text, this idea that there is someone with a key to your game is interesting.

The Anti-You theory can be summed up like this. You've just arrived at the academy and you are getting changed or taking your sandals off when that gnawing feeling starts in your gut. You hope Big Dave doesn't show up, then you can have a few easy rolls and a few hard but technical rolls but if Dave shows up then you know crushing defeat beckons. It will be in the form of a guard pass and high-pressure side control or horror-of-horrors a submission. The fact that Dave is a lower rank (sometimes he's the same rank but rarely higher ranked) is beside the point. No matter what you do he has your game book in his pocket. He is your personal kryptonite.

You walk out of changing and ... crap, there's Dave just walked in, shaking hands with everyone and smiling. That mofo knows he has me already. You know you'll try but Dave will apply some pressure and pass as sure as you just showed up for your beat down.

Of course, Big Dave is fictitious, and a metaphorical representation of your own Dave - the Anti-You. We all have them. I have one (even two) that were the same rank as me and no matter what I did I could not get the upper hand. If the 'upper hand' is what we are calling working our game. The opportunity to submit these guys was laughable, and these guys knew it. Once Keith explained the principle of the Anti-You and that BJJ was a great way to break this stupid pattern then I felt liberated. Only slightly but now I knew I wasn't alone, I thought it was just me that had an Anti-You.

I bet even your Professor has an Anti-You. If he competes, I dare say he goes for team training before a big tournament. There will be someone there that is his Anti-You. It will be someone who has his game; I've even seen Black Belts with Brown Belt Anti-You versions. The brown belts looks like phenoms, they are fearless against these black belts and then when you get a chance to roll with them and start wondering when you'll need to tap and you find they aren't exactly special? What's that all about?

With me, it was about confidence. I had given my power to my Anti-You, Big Dave had my number, his Gi was woven with the finest kryptonite to sap my super powers. Once I embarked on the thirty-day program though I took Keith's advice and rolled with Big Dave whenever I got the chance. At first, within the first couple of weeks, no change. He ate me for breakfast, yet lesser players subbed him with no issue. Sooooo frustrating.

Then a break appeared, a chink in the armor. We were doing specific training and I was on bottom but the technique we were working just so happened to be part of my map and I had drilled this technique heavily. Oops! I swept him and took his back. This was going against the grain and even Dave realized it. He thrashed but I was in a real comfortable position. I didn't get the sub though.

None of that mattered ... the spell was broken. It's like a fighter who is invincible; they have an unbeaten record - undefeated. Undefeated does not mean undefeatable. Once the armor cracks nothing is the same after that. I can work my game with confidence and it's effective against him, since then I think he might have achieved his goal maybe once and I've got a 99% success rate. I planned the work then worked the plan. I now have a different Anti-You, but he's a much higher rank ... a higher target to reach.

The Anti-You is healthy, don't be intimidated by your Anti-You. In fact, the opposite should be true, seek him (or her) out. They are the mirror that you need to break, this will break your game to a different level, remember Big Dave is essential to your growth.

THE DOOR OPENS BOTH WAYS

This is one of the more controversial subjects regarding BJJ and one that I feel strongly about. You must consider this information for what it is: Information. I have no opinion either way regarding the history and roots of Brazilian Jiu Jitsu and how this affects the way you train. I personally believe that if you consider this idea and have the kahunas to try it then your confidence and your game will improve.

The concept behind the 'Door Swings' is that you should train at another academy at least once per month. If you can, make it a non-local school. If you are on vacation then train where you are, if you are local then find another school that has drop-in fees or allows drop-in workouts and then go train there. The door to your academy allows you to walk in but it also allows you to walk out.

To me this is a very freeing concept. A lot of BJJ professors will probably be horrified, I know some of the older ones (usually Brazilian) really dislike this idea while some of the younger more forward thinking professors (still Brazilian) encourage it. In fact, if your school is part of a larger association like Alliance or Gracie Barra then why not train at another one of those schools in the network that is out of town, even if it's just once a month?

Why is this important? I first came across this mode of training when I was traveling through Europe. Looking for a BJJ school I found one on the Internet and then tracked down the schedule, saw they had Gi Jiu Jitsu so I grabbed my stuff and went along.

It was a shambles. The school owner turned up half an hour late; I was still in the parking lot in the rain. He told me there's no fee but that it's not Gi training anymore. He runs a stable of MMA fighters who have fights coming up in a couple of weeks, but I was okay to train with them if that was okay with me. I agreed and went in. The place was a toilet, rain was coming in, the mat was damp, mold everywhere and the stench of body odor was almost visible. Along one wall hung a few Gi jackets, with accompanying white belts alongside. The instructor (who looked like a wrestling coach) told me that due to their affiliation outside of the IBJJF that they didn't have promotions and most of the guys had been training for years. Great, I now had no idea of the rank of the guys I would be rolling with. There was half a cage set up in a corner and I was told to warm up over there, inside the half cage, out of the way.

While I'm doing jumping jacks, pushups, etc. some of the squad started coming in. All I saw was over-muscled Vee-shapes, mohawks, tattoos and giant thick necks. Not one of them acknowledged me, preferring to vent their shitty day by raging against the hanging bags dotted around the periphery of the room. I just carried on with the jumping jacks, surrounded by these white Mr. T.'s all laughing at each others 'in' stories and giving me sideways glances.

The instructor called them into a huddle where he announced what the order of training was going to be, then he told them "This guy just got here from America, he wants to roll with you all, so give him a good time." I held up my hand in a 'Hi' kind of gesture. I could have swore I heard someone growl.

No one came near me. They started to roll light with each other to warm up, within the first ten minutes the nurse needed to be called for one guys snapped fingers. Then one of the Mr. T's came over, "You wanna roll?" What could I say, I was there to roll. Bearing in mind that I had not trained any No-Gi in a number of years I still told him, "Sure."

He told me to remove my Gi jacket, he was purely a No-Gi type of guy, so I duly obliged. We touched knuckles and away we went, and this is why it is important to train at other establishments.

The energy is different and you also get a feel for other styles of Jiu Jitsu. Unlike most other martial arts that have distinct styles, BJJ is supposed to be a similar format regardless of the school, as all roads ultimately lead back to Carlos or Helio. But different schools teach different ways and on my travels I have come across some BJJ schools that teach only self defense and don't engage in any type of competitive techniques and vice versa. This is good and expands your sense of where you are in your Jiu Jitsu game. The energy is different in different schools and academies, and you need to feel that.

Back to my 'fish-out-of-water' roll. He pushed me into a position where I was very comfortable, he tried to pass and I swept him. This was okay, he told me, "I'm super-comfortable on my back." He held me in half guard, I escaped then he went for a kimura. Whoopsie! I spun and got the armbar and the tap.

He grinned, rubbed inside his elbow, we touched knuckles and off we went again. I assumed he had just made a mistake. We went through this dance for ten minutes, he had around twenty pounds on me in muscle weight and I had only been off a sixteen hour flight a couple of hours. I tapped him four times and pushed him into positions at will. The reality did not match my imagination, I thought I was about to be ritually murdered, but it just didn't happen, the fundamentals of my Jiu Jitsu did not allow it to happen.

We stopped, he was really happy and asked me how I passed a particular guard move he had, we discussed it and I showed him how I did it. He was stoked that he had learned a new technique. I was exhausted though and felt like I was about to pass out when another one of the guys much smaller came over grinning and asked if we could go. Again I said 'Sure', and off we went, this time with the Gi.

He was much more technical and more challenging and it was a good enjoyable roll with some good sweeps and positions on both sides, no subs. He wore a white belt but clearly wasn't. Again the energy was different, the style was different, but it proved in both cases that 'my' Jiu Jitsu worked here as well as anywhere else. This was a massive confidence boost to me.

We rolled some more and the instructor asked about a couple of the sweeps I had caught his students with and we discussed them, then we drilled a couple of the moves. When the class came to a close I had ten new best friends. This is how Jiu Jitsu works. Don't come in with an ego; leave that somewhere else, and you will leave with new knowledge and newfound friends.

I saw a cool quote on a poster recently: Your opponent is your best professor and your ego is your worst enemy.

Training at other schools really puts that to the test. This is how I see it. If you are consistently subbing the other students in your academy and just rolling with white belts for a rest you are not being challenged. It improves your technical ability, there is a downside to over-exposure of this kind though.

As it continues your ego becomes more fragile with each win, you feel good and the taste of defeat is an all but distant memory. Why put yourself in a position where you could be submitted or even have your guard passed when it's all cool right here in the comfort of your own academy?

You need to tap. It's that simple. Maybe when you are a third degree black belt and in the process of evolving techniques that other BJJ players want to emulate you might not need it. But if you are student looking to progress then the aim of the game is to tap 10,000 times. If you are the Big Fish then I bet it's a small pond. Swim out into the ocean, look for the whales, and get eaten alive. After a while this kind of training takes you back to the beginning, the origin of why you adopted BJJ as your sport of choice in the first place. Your True Home.

Finally, I want to mention why this seems such a big deal and has to do with the controversial topics of Teams and the expression Creonte. It's not unusual for an academy to belong to a team, some do, some don't, but the general consensus is the affiliation with one team or another. They are many and varied, always having a large presence at the various tournaments throughout the world especially the big ones like the Worlds, Pan Ams and Mundial.

To a degree being part of an association or a team is a good thing. The being part of a larger family than just your academy-family can bring a sense of belonging and bonding, also the chance to learn new techniques and share ideas with other team members. There is no escaping the reality though that Brazilian Jiu Jitsu is an individual sport. It's as individual as boxing or solo gymnastics, when the time comes to compete you can't call on your teammates to join in and help out. This isn't soccer or football, this is a one-on-one activity, when the ship sails you're the captain. Period.

The Team idea I think comes from the Brazilian culture it was born in. Just like the affiliation and association to soccer teams where people would die rather than support another team and this ideal has slid into Jiu Jitsu - it didn't slip into Japanese Jiu Jitsu.

This is very different than most other martial arts cultures. Sure, you see Karate/Taekwondo/Judo schools cheering on their teammates from their own school but you won't see such a deep affiliation or identity with a team. You seldom see banners flying and large blocks of cheering individuals wearing the same tee-shirt. It just doesn't occur to them, and then again it's not usual even in Eastern culture for teams to be cheered anyway.

If you go and train at another school that is not part of your team you might want to have a travel Gi (a nondescript Gi from a general manufacturer with no team patches on), this is what I do. Then when I show up, I use my regular belt so I'm not sand bagging anyone and I usually tell the professor or coach my affiliation but outside of that no one would know which team or association/school I belong to. Why? Because I'm looking to roll and test my skills, not get assassinated. A lot of BJJ student identify so strongly with their team that a member of another team coming along to 'play' would be an affront to their identity and ego.

This leads to some pretty tough rolls if you wear your team Gi, it took a whisper in my ear from an older and wiser team mate to let me know that it's not cool to train at other schools while flying the flag of your own team. I got his point. Training at one school while traveling one of the students punched me in the eye as soon as we touched knuckles then laughed, as did his 'teammates'. This to me is complete bullshit. In a sport where we are trying to stop bullying, we do this by bullying other students because they are not part of our team? It stinks!

Training at another academy does not make you a Creonte (the Brazilian expression for traitor). I'm sure that's not the literal meaning, though it could be, but that's what I have always believed it to be when I've heard it mentioned. If you are Brazilian and this is part of your culture then it is totally understandable. If you are not Brazilian then what the hell are you thinking?!

This is about as cultural to a non-Brazilian as asking the manager of 24 Hour Fitness if it's okay if you train at Big Box Fitness down the street. It just wouldn't happen, and if the manager at 24 Hour confronted you about your disloyalty to his gym after working out at Big Box, you would tell him where to get off. This doesn't appear to be the case with a lot of students who are worried that they will be labeled 'Creonte'.

Go and train elsewhere. You pay your membership fee to your academy, you are their customer and not the other way round. Test your skills. See if your brown, purple or blue belt stands up to the pressure of another academy, you'll find out pretty quick. I promise.

© DC Comics Warner

FREESTYLE ZEN JIU JITSU

This chapter title is probably as controversial as the Team / Creonte issue. It's a philosophy that has come to fruition due to competitors like Jeff Glover, Caio Terra, the Mendes Bros., Braulio Estima, Ribeiro Bros., to name only a few. They are all parts of teams but they believe Jiu Jitsu to be an open-ended education, they are evolving in this endless supply of technique opportunities. In fact recently I heard that Glover doesn't call his style Brazilian Jiu Jitsu anymore but 'Fun Jiu Jitsu'. That to me sounds like a training session I would enjoy. I have nothing against the Brazilian word per se, and they are instrumental in the development of the Japanese art, but I also feel that we can call it Jiu Jitsu now and people will know what you do. You could argue that the layman could become confused and think that we practice the Japanese form of the art, and my answer to that is 'So What?' The original art form is as valid as the BJJ School that only practices self-defense.

The type of student I see reading this manual is more the sport-based combatant than self-defense oriented, as the book does make the claim to improve your game in 30 days and not maim someone in 30 days. Let's face, we could maim someone in 30 seconds regardless of whether we are a sport or self defense practitioner.

The point of this chapter is to ask the student to open his mind. I suppose that means you.

This is from the Blog of Joe Lewis, the Karate phenom in the 60's, 70's and 80's. He trained with Bruce Lee and people always ask him about the experience, here is one answer: "Bruce [Lee] was working in 1968 and '69 an attempt to avoid all the excessive "trapping" his practitioners were using as an attribute of that system. This was many of the changes Bruce was working on; remember, he was still young and in his twenties. Imagine what changes he would advocate today had he remained alive."

You might ask, if Bruce Lee had lived where would martial arts be today ... including BJJ? As a side note, Chuck Norris is a Brown Belt in BJJ from the Machado brothers? The legacy still lives.

Don't limit yourself. Your Professor is your original source, ask him questions, and take some privates. Ask his advice about your Map and the positions you are planning to make your own, he may think it's a little early for the tornado guard. He may also think that it would suit your game to perfection. But don't limit yourself.

This is the Ethos of American Freestyle Jiu Jitsu. This is what happens when you get your Jiu Jitsu, add in some wrestling, find a cool Aikido technique and drill the hell out of the combination. You think Eddie Bravo cares what you (or any Gracie's) think of his moves? He doesn't seem to care from the *Truck* to the *Electric Chair*! You need to open your mind and try new stuff; this is only possible though when you spend a lot of time on the mat. You can't come up with a tornado guard combo when you only train twice a week, and I don't care if you are a black belt training twice a week: the expansive positions and techniques will evade you.

WORKAROUNDS

CAN'T GET TO THE STUDIO OR ACADEMY AT YOUR REGULAR TIME?

If you can't get to your academy as part of your regular program then plan your day beforehand with class built in as an appointment. If you know you are going to be working late then see if you can grab a lunchtime session. This is only usually necessary within the 30-day process. If you are traveling, look to see which schools are in that area, and don't forget your Travel Gi.

GOING ON VACATION?

Look for local academies where you finally land. Remember the earlier story about traveling through Europe, I facebooked academies and schools as my itinerary suggested and found that I could pretty much find a school to train at while being constantly on the move. Some schools will be very different and only practice self-defense and some schools will only practice drilling or competition class. Try and adapt. It's good for your BJJ.

WHAT IF I'M SICK?

Rest. But don't fall apart. One of the important things to know is that you can start and restart the 30-day process at any time. The fact that you didn't get all the 30-day process down first time out the gate doesn't matter. I guarantee if that all you managed to get through was 14 days before the flu hit or whatever, that you will be better than you were at the beginning. You just need to periodize your training.

If you are resting I strongly recommend buying some DVD's and reviewing techniques then visualizing them. This is a very powerful process to improvement. Can you stand another story?

When I was a new blue belt I loved training so much I couldn't keep away from the academy. We had a new professor from Brazil come to train and coach at our place, a current World Champ and a great technician. I couldn't get enough of his classes. Then after a roll I showed a medical surgeon who was part of the class that I had this rash forming on my collarbone that wouldn't heal. He took a look, made a face then gave me a business card for a skin doctor. I'm thinking staph, I was wrong it was cancer! Two different forms and I needed two surgeries right away.

The first surgery left me with a nine-inch stitch line that went from my collarbone to my breastbone. It was horrible too, real gnarly. The next one scooped a series of lumps of skin from the base of my neck. All was good; I was recovering well but with wounds that could bust open at any minute, training was out. In fact, I was out for sixteen weeks! That's right - four months.

As soon as I didn't need the pain meds so much, I began walking on a treadmill. I felt very weak and looked pale and thin. Bed rest was important as so much skin had been removed the flesh on my pectorals was extremely tight, reaching for something without it feeling like my skin would tear open was a very real experience. Plus the painkillers were super strong, for the first four weeks I was in a constant stupor.

When I felt well enough, I would sit up in bed and watch a couple of YouTube videos. Then a friend of mine grabbed me a copy of the Jeff Glover Deep Half Guard DVD to lift my spirits.

At my stage of development I had never really used a Deep Half so it was really interesting. I began to watch it a lot and study it over and over. Fed up with daytime TV, there was nothing else to watch. As part of the treadmill work I would try and slowly move into some of the positions Jeff Demonstrated. He also did some moves with a huge inflatable ball as a drilling practice. I tried those too.

But the real breakthrough came when I visualized myself back at training and sweeping people with the moves I was watching. I had this daydream over and over.

The day finally came when I could go back to training. Naturally I was a little concerned I was out of shape (which I was, my cardio was non-existent) my training partners were sympathetic and took it easy with me. What amazed them though was I was moving into the Deep Half position with ease, and then pulling off the sweeps. One of my teammates said, "Sure you even had time out? You seem to better than before you left." This was interesting to say the least. Now if I have any downtime or I'm periodizing I make sure to watch videos last thing at night just before I go to sleep, this somehow sinks the technique into my subconscious. Give it a try.

I CAN'T AFFORD A SUBMISSION DUMMY ... OR MATS!

These aren't essential. They are just easier and more convenient. Especially if you must periodize your training between white belt classes and advanced classes. If you are a white belt then practice the moves on the carpet in the lounge: shrimping, half guard and guard positions, etc.

If you can get yourself a training-partner, even better. I'm very motivated and earn a good living so having a dummy is very convenient for me and I can afford it. This is the best option if you want to practice and drill techniques at home. If it's out of your reach though, see if one of your team members wants to drill techniques for an hour once a week. I asked my Professor (before Burt the dummy arrived) if a friend and me could practice some techniques on a Saturday morning before the kids' class. He was fine with it, so my buddy drilled what he wanted and I drilled what I wanted. It worked; you've just got to get creative.

If you can't afford mats then stick to the mats at the academy. If you have a dummy, you don't necessarily need mats you can still drill in the lounge on carpet or a rug like a lot of people do.

My advice though is don't use grass. It's unsanitary and if you wear a Gi it will be ruined in no time with grass stains and crap. If you have a limited budget and still want mats, but on the cheap, then go online and look up gymnastic tumbling mats. You can get them really low-cost, as gymnastics and kids practicing at home is big, whereas Jiu Jitsu is a little more niche and the online stores know it. You won't be able to do shoulder throws, take downs, etc.

as gym mats are little thinner at 1-1/2" rather than 2" for most BJJ mats but they do the job admirably. You can probably cover a 10' x 10' area for a couple hundred bucks and they store really easy, as they are lightweight.

As a side note, if you don't have a dummy, don't practice on your kids or the dog. Mine get pissed off real quick if I just want to 'try' something on them.

FORGOT MY BJJ JOURNAL?

Use your phone. Most smartphones come with a notebook, jot your roll down there and then transfer it when you get to your journal. And don't forget to use some video recording while you are at it.

CHAPTER FOUR: COMPETITION PSYCHOLOGY IN BRIEF

It's not the point of this text to provide complete competition psychology. It is an important part of the whole psyche of BJJ training. There are better books more suited to handling the 'head case' side of competing. I strongly recommend 'Roadmap to the Zone' by Robert S.Neff, Ph.D. And Michael K. Garza, Ed.D.

This covers the various elements that go into mental preparation for a tournament, and includes but is not limited to:

- Creating a Map
- Visualization
- Positive Self Talk
- Emotions and Zoning
- The Emotion Wheel

I will cover the Zoning technique that I use next:

ZONING

To keep in the Zone while you are training you can often use a technique called the Refocus Ritual (RR). I use this usually when my game isn't working for some reason. If I am trying to get into positions and getting stuffed or my timing is off then I need to refocus and get my game back together.

If you are competing this is an excellent way to refocus between matches too. For the most part I force the game to stop and then refocus during the roll, if I am in the academy. In a tournament I use this RR when the ref returns us to a position, for example, if we are rolling out of bounds or need to redress, *especially if we need to redress.*

In the academy, I will purposefully roll towards other rolling partners, so the coach stops us, or into a wall, off the mat, anything to pause the action. This gives me just enough time to regroup and fix what's going on. If my game is plugged in, then I still use the RR to reinforce this feeling but I don't force the pause in the action. I only do it when I get the sub or my opponent needs to stop due to the usual pause practices mentioned above.

Here is my RR.

As soon as a pause is effected:
1.   Turn my back to my opponent.
2.   Untie my belt (unless its already off) - focus on my hands being soft doing this to relax my grips and forearms.
3.   Control my eyes, I dangle the belt to the ground to get it even before retying it.
4.   As I tie it I breathe and relax, I even internally say to myself 'Relax and Breathe'.
5.   I mentally prepare for how I want to pick the game up. Which guard I plan to use or which reversal, escape, etc.

These days this isn't even a conscious thought process, I have done it so many times. The only thing I am now consciously aware of is the internal sounding of the word 'relax' and preparing in my mind for the next position. If you want to give it a try use this rhyme to remember the process.

'Untie the belt, Control the eyes, Breathe, Relax and Visualize.'

CHAPTER FIVE: WHY ZEN?

This is Zen Buddhism as described by David Tuffley in his treatise on Buddhism: The Essence of Buddhism. I think that it encapsulates this manual on Zen Jiu Jitsu and the ethos behind it very well:

'Buddhism is not a religion as such; and does not propose an external God. It does not seek to replace any persons existing religious beliefs, only to supplement them. The Buddha, in all likelihood, would rather his followers describe themselves simply as *Followers of the Way*.'

This is how I feel and Jiu Jitsu is the Way.

CHAPTER SIX: FOLLOW THROUGH

'It is one thing to study war and another to live a warriors life.'
~ Telamon of Arcadia, Mercenary of the fifth century B.C.

MOTIVATION & PLATEAUS

Staying motivated for the long haul in any sport is one of the most challenging areas. There are times when your exuberance just isn't as high as it once was, it's hard to keep the excitement and hunger chugging along.

I understand. These are usually very personal times when we can't seem to get No Satisfaction whatever we try and training seems like a chore. You get a down or a low feeling when training time comes around and anything from walking the dog to doing the dishes seems like a better option. This can be caused due to a multitude of reasons and there are many ways in which you can be over-trained, these are discussed in the section on Burnout, but staying Motivated is highly important ... if not essential in your progression to Black Belt.

Using your journal to track progress and keep you on track can be helpful. Using goals to move you into better positions and learning new positions can keep you motivated too.

One of the best motivational devices in my opinion is the opportunity to learn. We all like to learn cool moves. If you don't like to learn cool moves then I would question what attracted you to BJJ in the first place. If you are feeling a little on the low side and are maybe using the Overtraining Avoidance techniques from the Burnout section then it can be a good idea to look for a couple of techniques or guard plays that you like the look of. Analyze the techniques and then find a way to apply them to your own game. If you have a sub dummy take a couple of classes off and just play with the dummy for twenty to thirty minutes. Don't push it, just play.

The timing here is important. Some students' try and blast through this period thinking that more is better, actually it's the other way around. Dial everything back and make the process manageable, but don't stop.

This is a story I heard about a great tennis coach and how he rehabilitated one of his students back from serious health problems all the way to state champion. The kid was bed ridden but the coach went along anyway and talked to him each day, then one day he said, okay let's pull the covers back and take a look at those legs. The student obliged. The next day he did the same but lifted one leg slightly, the next day much of the same but lifted the other leg. Over time he moved the kid around and got him to swing his legs off the bed, always returning him to his bed ridden state. Eventually, he could stand then walk then run then run fast and play tennis.

You'll notice that the coach didn't turn up, throw the blankets back and say 'come on son, let's get jogging, the State Champs are coming up.' It's funny though, that's the way a lot of BJJ students look at a funk: pile it on; push through it, like a seasoned Marine. Even Marines know when to dial it back and live to fight another day and even if they don't their commanders do.

But don't stop. The idea of taking a break from training is very appealing but remember the old workouts at the gym. You don't feel like it one night and then you tell yourself you'll catch up tomorrow. How did that work out? It doesn't matter if you drag yourself to the academy and get tapped by a ton of white belts. Show up.

You'll slide out of the plateau when your mind adjusts to the new techniques and level you are at. The mind and body connection are important in BJJ and a lot of students misunderstand this. There is a direct connection. Sometimes this connection gets out of sync and we get the impression that we are getting worse. It's happened to me a few times when I wanted to call it quits. On reassessment the 30-

day program became a reality and I now enjoy my Jiu Jitsu more then ever.

I forget to reassess from time to time. It's very important, more important than you can imagine, that your training log and journal act as motivational tools for future development. If you feel your fire for training dropping in temperature then get your journal out and reassess. There will be some high notes in there, and some positions that really got you excited, revisit them. See what blows your hair back, and then drill some of those techniques.

Keep looking for new techniques that suit your game too. <u>Do not drill or practice every technique that comes along</u> that will only lead to some form of confusion. You need to think, my side control could be tighter/better/stronger, then go seek the antidote to this. As part of the Zen Jiu Jitsu program we will be developing maps for various positions, but until they are ready you will have to figure out where you want your game to be.

A friend of mine is a crazy competitor. I reckon if there were a tournament locally every week, he would compete every week. He goes into tournaments too that are way past his pay-grade and he gets murdered in the first round. Still, I can't help but admire his grit and spunk. Lately though, I've seen the 'look' on his face. This is the look of disillusionment, the look of burnout. This has happened before, I've seen the 'look' on many students faces, most of the time these guys change academies (literally changing teams) thinking that this is going to change their results in the tournament standings. For the most part they wash out of Jiu Jitsu, which is a crying shame. They would have been better served to take a short break, ease back into training by drilling some techniques that could ignite the spark again.

If you feel like you are giving the 'look' to your fellow training partners. Go into the 30-day program as prescribed here. If you feel low on energy or weak, the adjustment to make is to install the first two-week (at least) as all LI training sessions. A mixture of fundamentals and drilling with some light sparring that should do the trick. Regroup. Come back stronger. This strategy is a winner.

IN CONCLUSION

What does this all mean?

It's not rocket science. It's a thirty-day program that asks you to make Jiu Jitsu part of your every day life for a month. It asks you to mix the plan between hi-intensity and low-intensity and drill specific moves related to the game you want to improve upon then record it.

Hope you can handle another Bruce Lee quote:
"In building a statue, a sculptor doesn't keep adding clay to his subject. Actually, he keeps chiseling away at the inessentials until the truth of its creation is revealed without obstructions. Thus, contrary to other styles, being wise in Jeet Kune-Do doesn't mean adding more; it means to minimize, in other words to hack away the unessential. It is not daily increase but daily decrease; hack away the unessential."

You have to take from this manual what you need. Don't just keep adding techniques or positions for the sake of adding. In fact, listen to Bruce: subtract. Take away the mistakes; keep the details that work for you. Drill your A-Game.

Too much emphasis these days is placed on tournament wins. Tournaments should be a part of every BJJ player to enhance and expand their game, to test the process and technique. This is not the end, only the means.

A good BJJ player should be balanced; the perfect state of mind is mentally controlled precision. The 'calm in the midst of the storm' this is the pinnacle of Jiu Jitsu technique. A coach of mine always says if you get into a street situation and it continues, the longer it carries on; the odds improve in your favor. Why is this? Because Jiu Jitsu is based totally on the virtue of patience. You must turn up for training, and learn as much on the mats as you can. It doesn't get much more complex than that.

If you have enjoyed this book then go back to the beginning and re-read it, or just dip into sections that we covered that piqued your interest, especially the thirty-day protocol. I hope you enjoyed this journey as much I did putting it together. It was an education for me too. If you have any comments, additions or ideas, please get in touch via my website at:

http://jiujitsubuddha.com

I would love to hear from you and your thoughts on the concepts and ideas discussed. Maybe we'll meet on the mat some day, I very much look forward to it.

Be water, my friend.

CHAPTER SEVEN: RESOURCES AND REFERENCE

MORE BOOKS
Zen Jiu Jitsu - Beyond Rolling
Zen Jiu Jitsu Training Log
Zen Jiu Jitsu - White to Blue
Zen Jiu Jitsu - Over 40

REFERENCES:
University of Jiu Jitsu. Saulo Ribeiro and Kevin Howell. Victory Belt Publishing 2008
Outliers. Malcolm Gladwell. Back Bay Books 2011
Roadmap to the Zone. Robert S Neff Ph.d. And Michael K Garza Ed.D. Authorhouse 2004
2012 World Jiu Jitsu Championships Case Study. BishopBjj.com
The Essence of Buddhism. David Tuffley. Kindle Edition 2011
Joe Lewis Fighting Systems

RECOMMENDED READING:
University of Jiu Jitsu. Saulo Ribeiro and Kevin Howell. Victory Belt Publishing 2008
Roadmap to the Zone. Robert S Neff Ph.d. And Michael K Garza Ed.D. Authorhouse 2004
Jiu Jitsu Unleashed. Eddie Bravo. McGraw-Hill 2005
The X Guard. Marcelo Garcia with Eric Krauss and Glen Cordoza. Victory Belt Publishing 2008.
The Cauliflower Chronicles. Marshal D Carper. Victory Belt Publishing 2010

RECOMMENDED WATCHING:
Jeff Glovers Deep Half Guard. Cryo Productions 2009
Saulo Ribeiro Jiu Jitsu Revolution. Series 1 and 2.
Robson Moura. Fusion 1 and 2.

111 Half Guard Techniques with Caio Terra. Cryo Productions 2011
Caio Terra Modern Jiu Jitsu. Mobile Black Belt 2012
Fight Club. 20th Century Fox. 2002.

RECOMMENDED WEBSITES:

http://bjjtech.com/tech/
http://bishopbjj.com
http://fightlogmedia.com
http://www.igrapple.com
http://www.grapplingdummy.net
http://armbarsoap.com
http://youtu.be/CWgke2m__6Y
http://youtu.be/4JsEOI5sLRM
http://youtu.be/KilhUNQ6r7U
http://www.joelewisfightingsystems.com
http://tapordiecompany.com

EXCERPT FROM ZEN JIU JITSU - WHITE TO BLUE

Core Principles

The Tap
"Cry in the Dojo. Laugh on the Battlefield."
~ Unknown - But Makes Perfect Sense.

There is one thing that makes Brazilian Jiu Jitsu unique compared to other martial arts and that is the Tap or Tap-Out. I don't want to get into any MMA or branding issues about the use of the word TapOut so we'll refer to it here as the Tap.

When you find yourself in a position that you feel (if you continued) may cause you harm then the simple tap-tap on your partners arm, anywhere on his body, the mat or even a verbal tab (sometimes required when you are bent into a position that makes a hand or foot tap impossible) the match or sparring session stops. This is used mostly in sparring and is the greatest advantage over any other martial art.

And what an advantage...
This gives all BJJ practitioners the opportunity to spar full contact, going hard and still not hurting each other. How many other contact sports can boast such a claim. The Tap is the most powerful element in Jiu Jitsu and should not be considered a weakness, as my own professor tells me, "You have to tap a thousand times before you can consider yourself a black belt." He actually uses the mechanism of tapping to keep score of his level of improvement.

Only last week I was rolling with a very good black belt. I was a lot heavier and moved myself into a dominant position. He was telling me not to be so nice and get moving into the submission position. Heeding his words I moved and after a long (and patient) process I eventually managed a tap. When we reset he fixed his Gi and asked me why I was being so nice. I sort of shrugged, I didn't have an answer, maybe I am too nice, maybe I am too respectful of higher-ranking belts.

Who knows? This is when he hit me with the thunderbolt that made a great connection. "You cannot hurt me. All I need to do is tap." And he tapped me twice on the shoulder to prove his point. This was him giving me permission to go on the attack. In this sport whether you are attacking or defending you are learning something. It does not benefit you or your partner to go easy, unless it's a light roll by mutual consent or there is a huge disparity in weight, age or rank.

Don't imagine that because a new white belt on his third class at the academy knows how to tap then he's open season. That's not why we're here. But if you put the newbie in pressure positions and help him to look for escapes while trying to submit, then you BOTH improve. If you get in a tough spot with a higher-ranking belt or heavier opponent know this: There is no disgrace in tapping.

In fact, if you are just rolling with a buddy (same, weight, age and rank) and he catches you with a clean arm lock and you tap. How do you feel? Do you want to go kick the dog? Scream obscenities at him/her? Or are you proud that your buddy is coming along?

If it's kick the dog or scream then I fear your days as a long term BJJ fighter are truly numbered. This is part of the game and I'm super happy when one of my training partners catches me. If it keeps happening every session then I would talk to my professor or coach for an appropriate escape and the survival options. We'll talk more about those in a later section.

This is one of the reasons that Royce Gracie proved BJJ to be so effective in the original UFC 1. Don't forget this was a very different version of the UFC than what is represented today. This was when it was a game of styles, so Karate would go against Boxing, or Taekwondo against Sumo. Weights and ages etc. were of no consequence, it was all about styles. So little one hundred and seventy five pound Royce would be put against two hundred and fifty pound beasts. And not just for three rounds, this was as long as it took and then after each round he would fight a different opponent until there was one winner. It was true gladiator style back then - bloody and brutal.

Royce though had a secret weapon though...the tap.

He had been training full on sparring all his life. He used leverage to his advantage in real life situations and no-holds-barred matches. The other styles didn't have this capability. Think about it, how could a boxer, taekwondo fighter, muay thai guy or karate stylist go 100 % each sparring session without getting brain damage?

Even if they were strikers that went hard they were always padded up to some degree with gloves, headgear, body armor so when the time came to go all out against an opponent then it was a different experience. They could not spar for real.

Not so for Royce. He had been rolling in the Gi and tapping (and being tapped) since he was kid. He went into the Octagon pulled these poor unsuspecting souls to the canvas and submitted them, to him it was just playing around. This is all seems so matter-of-fact today, but before the world had become exposed to Jiu Jitsu no one had ever seen anything like this.

At the time, this must have been a shocking realization for a lot of the other styles who believed that they were the deadliest men on the planet. The original line-up (and many others in years to come) would tell anyone who would listen that they were real bad-asses. Then they hit Royce Gracie and came up short.

This wasn't achieved because Jiu Jitsu had some secret techniques passed down from Shaolin Monks in a remote Tibetan cave. It was all because Royce could train full contact <u>all the time,</u> and that was only because of the tap.